CONTENTS

LIST OF FIGURES

LIST OF TABLES

PREFACE

Our aim in this book is to provide, for non-planning students, and for other lay readers, an outline of the essential characteristics of the role and context of the British system of town and country planning. Our aim is not to provide an exhaustive and detailed treatment of planning law and policy, but to provide the non-specialist with an understanding of the practice and limitations of planning within the contemporary geography of Britain's social and economic environment. This understanding seems pressing in the face of the current crisis of confidence in the planning profession itself. It is also needed by the politicians who employ town and country planners in central and local government and by the general public, who are often vociferously aware of 'planning disasters' such as 'heartless' city centres and 'soul-less' tower blocks, while being unaware of the careful regulation of development which has often preserved amenity rather than destroyed it.

Planning is an ill-defined collection of practices and policies which have their conceptual roots in a variety of circumstances. In some instances they are the explicit fruit of well articulated ideology, while in others they stem simply from the sheer necessity to ameliorate unsatisfactory living conditions. Our concern here is with the modern situation, but current application of planning policies incorporates an evolution of practice and theory which has developed over the years in response to the changing needs and perceptions of society, and this, too, adds to the untidiness of the system.

Essentially, we are concerned in Part One to identify the basic machinery of the planning system, its organisation and application at the various scales of operation. In Part Two we seek to evaluate the scope and the success of planners in the main sectors of their activities and in the face of the major problems of the day. As will become apparent, both scope and success are variable commodities, due partly to the ambiguous position of planning in a mixed economy but more often to the unpredictability and uncontrollability of a national economy that is so inextricably enmeshed with world events on the one hand, and incapable of being disaggregated into local economies on the other.

ACKNOWLEDGEMENTS

The authors are pleased to acknowledge the assistance of S Pratt in the compilation of artwork for this book.

Thanks are also due to the following for permission to use copyright material in figures or in tables:

Mid-Glamorganshire CC (2.4), Leeds City Council (2.5a), Derby City Council (2.5b), Kirklees Metropolitan Council (2.6, 8.1, 8.2), Darlington Borough Council (3.5), Gloucestershire CC (Table 8), Lewes District Council (Table 18), Yorkshire Dales National Park Committee (Table 19), English Tourist Board (5.2), Manpower Services Commission (4.1), Crown Copyright Sources (Crown Copyright Reserved) (3.1, 3.2, 5.1, 5.3, 6.1) A W McMillen, Traffic Engineering Control (6.2), P Jones, Estates Gazette (7.3), D T Cross and M R Bristow, Pion Ltd (9.1), M J Bruton, Town Planning Review (Table 7) M S Gibson and M J Langstaff, Hutchinson Ltd, (Table 10), G Shaw, Service Industries Review (Table 17), Planning (Table 20), The Planner (7.2), Dyfed County Council (Table 2), Cleveland County Council (Table 13).

NOTE: The extracts from statutory and other plans included in this book are used as examples only and should not necessarily be regarded as the current policies of the authorities concerned.

INTRODUCTION

Town and country planning as we have come to know it in Britain is a relatively recent development, signified by the fact that its definition, 'the organisation of the lay-out or design of buildings, the development of land etc.', first occurred in the Addendum to the Shorter Oxford English Dictionary published as late as 1974. The youth of British planning may seem strange in the face of a tradition of architectural and urban design which stretches back over five thousand years, yet British planning, institutionalised by legislation and the emergence of a professional elite, is only a twentieth century phenomenon. Its immediate roots lie mainly in the radical structural changes which accompanied the industrial revolution; and it draws, severally, upon the need of communities to regulate their common life; the philanthropy of a few industrial entrepreneurs who wished to provide a higher standard of living conditions for their workers; and upon a political philosophy that drew, in turn, on the Utopian tradition.

Communities have always sought to regulate and order their functioning in some way or another. In Britain, the tradition of meetings of village elders and the establishment in towns of municipal corporations goes back to feudal times. Such bodies have customarily dealt with matters of the common good such as water supply, highways and the removal of effluents. Over the course of the nineteenth century, however, industrial change accompanied by a rapid rise in the density and agglomeration of the population made clear the need for systematic and contiguous local government. Under the 1888 Local Government Act the ad hoc system of municipal boroughs, county and parish government was replaced by a unified arrangement of County and County Borough Councils, the counties being further subdivided into urban and rural districts in 1894. Thus was provided a framework of democratically elected local bodies which, under the supervision of central government, could take on board existing sanitary and bye law regulation. From this base, local authorities have adopted the steadily more complex role of providing and maintaining the physical infrastructure, education and welfare facilities required for social and economic well being. Planning was a natural addition, tentatively developed in a series of Acts of Parliament and associated with the need to develop public sector housing, eg Housing and Town Planning Acts 1909 and 1919, the latter following on the heels of the 1918 Tudor Walters Report which advocated minimum standards of provision and greater public activity.

Local government has learned much, however, from the actions of a few energetic individuals. In the case of planning, it was largely the philanthropy of a few nineteenth century industrialists – Ackroyd, Salt and Crossley in West Yorkshire, followed by Lever in Cheshire and Cadbury in Birmingham – that promoted the creation of planned industrial communities recognisably modern in intention. Each of these Victorian capitalists sought to establish all the facilities they saw as necessary for social well being: decent houses, well laid out and substantial; open space for gardens, parks and informal recreation; shopping and community facilities such as churches, libraries and schools (although usually no licensed premises), all adjacent to their factories and laid out in an integrated fashion. The theme was well taken up by Ebenezer Howard in his book *Garden Cities of Tomorrow (1902)*. Howard advocated catering for urban growth by the creation of satellite communities which would be separated from the parent city by a stretch of open country. Here would be offered a completely new 'town-country' environment, the quality of which would be assured by the careful zoning of land uses and the maintenance of abundant grassy space. Howard helped to found and develop such a new town at Letchworth, 30 miles north of London, and in 1920 a further community, Welwyn Garden City. From such beginnings was laid down not just the concept of new towns, but a whole vocabulary of planning concepts and features, which has characterised British planning ever since (Table 1). To the initial concepts of *containment, decentralisation* and *segregation*, we can add *conservation* and *preservation* which were viewed at the time as largely countryside issues and the need for *renewal*, implicit in the Barlow Report (1940) at a regional scale, but made necessary at the city scale by the very success of the initial concepts as they were applied to practical planning in the post 1947 period.

Viewed in this light, British planning developed and has essentially remained a technical process of amelioration, to be undertaken by a disinterested professional elite. Yet Howard's creation of more ordered living conditions, like those of his predecessors, was part of his vision of an ordered society and planning owes something, therefore, to the aspirations of those who seek social and political change. By definition, planning has to do with the control of land use: such control has traditionally rested with land ownership and of course the ownership of land has been a key to political power since time immemorial. To the Socialist and Marxist, it is an axiom that land ownership should reside with the community and not with individuals. Over the present century British governments have periodically shared this left wing ideology, and in consequence have from time to time sought to implement policies designed to articulate such ideals. Most obviously was this the case with the 1947 Town and Country Planning Act which effectively laid the foundations of our present planning system.

The 1947 Act was the fruit of the most explicitly Socialist government Britain has ever had, and effectively nationalised the right to develop land. Henceforth landholders were obliged to seek planning permission from the local authority (county council or county borough council) for any new development. The newly designated *local planning authorities* were also to prepare Development Plans for their areas, indicating on Ordnance Survey maps what were considered to be appropriate zones of land use for the succeeding twenty years. *Development control* and the *development plan* have been the basic tools of planning ever since. The thorniest part of the 1947 legislation, however, dealt with the related aspects of the appropriation of development value by the state and the assembly of land from the private market for public purposes. The essential point is that once the state engages in a zoning policy, it affects the value of land and so interferes in the free market. The argument then runs that as the community has effectively designated the value of a plot of land, individuals should not profit simply from the fortuitous possession of land zoned for development (betterment), nor conversely, should they be penalised should land for which they had legitimate development expectation be zoned for other purposes (worsenment). The issue of personal profit at the expense of development

Table 1   Themes and Features in Planning's Vocabulary

CONTAINMENT	DECENTRALISATION	SEGREGATION
Greenbelt	Garden city/suburb	Zoning
Central business district	New Town	Residential suburb
Neighbourhood	Satellite town	Industrial estate
Key settlement	Overspill housing	Shopping centre
Country park	Regional centre	Open space
Access agreement		Pedestrianisation
		Ring road

CONSERVATION	PRESERVATION	RENEWAL
Amenity	Scheduled monument	Comprehensive redevelopment
National park	Listed building	Action area
Area of outstanding	Preservation order	Housing action area
natural beauty	Heritage coast	General improvement area
Conservation area	Site of special scientific	Inner city policy
Management agreement	interest	Enterprise Zone
		Urban development corporation

for community purposes e.g. a housing estate, is simply an extension of the matter. The 1947 Act instituted a 100% development charge so that profits which accrued to private owners from the development of land should pass to the state, and a once and for all fund to compensate those owners who were adversely affected by the Act. In the event the system stifled the land market, and being unacceptable to the succeeding Conservative government, was progressively dismantled and land was returned to a free market. Nevertheless, betterment lies at the heart of left wing views of planning and two successive Labour governments have tried to deal with the issue, only to have their legislation repealed either in whole or in part by following Conservative administrations. It is now generally accepted that some form of development tax is equitable, however, and the system introduced with the Labour 1976 Development Land Tax Act currently remains in force, although at rates lower than those originally set.

The period after 1945 saw unparalleled opportunities for planning. The 1947 Act, itself, was part of a suite of planning-related legislation including the 1945 *Distribution of Industry Act* which provided financial and infrastructure aid to industry in the newly designated development areas, the 1946 *New Towns Act* which gave national recognition to Howard's early vision and resulted in the designation of fourteen new towns by 1950, the 1946 and 1949 *Housing Acts* which introduced subsidies and low interest loans for local authority housing, and the 1949 *National Parks and Access to the Countryside Act*. Paradoxically, although the planned society envisaged by Labour was eschewed by the 1951 Conservative government, Labour's legislation, with the important exception of the betterment issue, was left largely intact. (Conservative housing policies favoured the private market, relegating council housing to those who could not afford to buy their own house, but the concept of local authority housing provision still remained to provide planners with an important opportunity to improve living conditions for a significant section of the population.) In effect, the political purposes of planning were somewhat set aside, and in the task of reconstruction and renewal after the war, made more urgent by the rising population, planning remained a largely technical exercise, responding to increasingly buoyant market forces, rather than directing them.

Yet inevitably, the operation of the planning system came to have political consequences. Containment and dispersal policies contributed to the increase of affluent suburban development beyond the existing fringes of the major cities, while new investment was diverted away from the inner urban areas, creating the seed bed of inner city decline. A more broadly based impact was made by the increasing degree of residential segregation, as the population was rehoused either in council or private estates. The well to do, in addition, were increasingly attracted to cherished countryside, leaving the less well off closest to the urban cores.

These features have persisted, even though in the 1960's there was a swing towards a more interventionist position by both Conservative and Labour governments. The emphasis, though, was on improving the *processes* of planning, rather than on evaluating the *purposes* of planning. While the planning system itself was overhauled, the techniques available changed, too. On the one hand, planners, armed with new tools of data analysis from the quantitative revolution in the social sciences, acquired a new confidence in their ability for social diagnosis and manipulation, while on the other, as architects embraced new building systems, the planners were provided with a means of rapid reconstruction in central business district and residential area alike. Planning appeared ascendant and the profession burgeoned, but its social impact proved in many places to be brutal and insensitive to both general amenity and personal needs. In consequence, the 1970's saw an increasing disatisfaction with the results of planning. The growing application of mechanistic social science began to be questioned more and more: the appalling maintenance costs of much high rise, high density housing hung like an albatross around the neck of planning. Within the profession questions as to the purposes of planning began to surface more frequently, and as the tide of economic recession began to rise, the ability of the planners to intervene was shown to be quite inadequate. Quite simply, insofar as planning rests upon development, if there is no development there can be little planning. By the early 1980's new private investment had virtually dried up outside a few favoured locations in the south of England, while government policies aimed at reducing public expenditure took away the opportunity for public-sector led development.

British planning, therefore, lies somewhat in the doldrums. After 70 years as an institutionalised profession (the Royal Town Planning Institute was founded in 1914), planners have a less than coherent view of their purpose. Yet without clearly defined national goals it is difficult for local planners to devise local strategies. Whereas in the 1960's there would at least have been a consensus that environmental improvement could be identified, planned for and engineered, that would be less so in the mid 1980's. A hard-line Conservative view might be that planning exists simply to facilitate the optimal operation of the land market, while a Labour view would be much more likely to emphasise the requirement of planning for regulating the land market.

Wherever the emphasis is to lie, however, planning has the task of reconciling competing claims for the use and development of limited land resources. This is principally achieved by regulating proposed development in the light of statutorily recognised plans that have the sanction of democratic approval. In the following pages we aim to simplify the complex matter of formulating those plans and their associated policies. Unfortunately, while it is relatively easy to identify the processes of planning, it will be seen that planning's purposes and degree of success are less obvious. Planning has undoubtedly had a significant impact on the development of the social and economic geography of Britain, but that impact has not always been what was intended, and while conceived often as a technical and spatial exercise, it has inevitably had political and social consequences.

Further reading

For a detailed review of the nineteenth century philanthropists see W L Creese 1966 *The Search for Environment* (Yale University Press). The most convenient overall review of planning's development is found in G Cherry 1974 *The Evolution of British Town Planning* (Leonard Hill), while for an introduction to a view of planning's purpose by a distinguished planner see D Eversley 1979 *The Planner in Society* (Faber). A wider context for British planning is provided by D H McKay, *Planning and Politics in Western Europe*, Macmillan, 1982.

PART ONE
THE INSTRUMENTS OF PLANNING

CHAPTER 1
THE GUIDING HAND OF CENTRAL GOVERNMENT

Although local planning is seen most frequently to be the concern of local planning authorities, central government exercises such close supervision of the system that it has been referred to as the key to land planning. The framework within which the entire system operates is laid down by statute determined by central government which now amounts to a mass of legislation, not all of which has been drafted with the specific end of town and country planning in mind (Fig 1.1). Such legislation may be:

mandatory	certain functions must be under-taken
discretionary	certain functions may be under-taken
enabling	certain functions may be under-taken in specific circumstances

Central control goes beyond the framing of the rules of planning, however, for central departments play a direct role in certain planning matters and exercise supervision over the activities of local planning authorities.

1.1 THE ORGANS OF POWER

Because planning relates to so many aspects of national life, it is influenced by the policies of many departments of state, and is served by a variety of fringe bodies and ad hoc groups. In addition, under the formal organisation discussed below, it is important to remember that there lies a web of political activity not only among Members of Parliament, but also between them and

Figure 1.1   Land Use Planning's Statutory Framework 1945–84

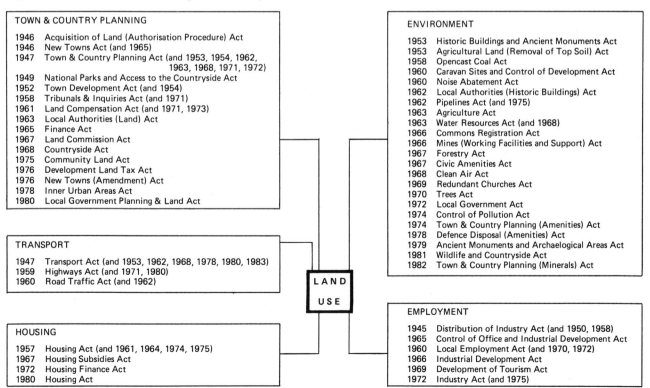

TOWN & COUNTRY PLANNING

1946	Acquisition of Land (Authorisation Procedure) Act
1946	New Towns Act (and 1965)
1947	Town & Country Planning Act (and 1953, 1954, 1962, 1963, 1968, 1971, 1972)
1949	National Parks and Access to the Countryside Act
1952	Town Development Act (and 1954)
1958	Tribunals & Inquiries Act (and 1971)
1961	Land Compensation Act (and 1971, 1973)
1963	Local Authorities (Land) Act
1965	Finance Act
1967	Land Commission Act
1968	Countryside Act
1975	Community Land Act
1976	Development Land Tax Act
1976	New Towns (Amendment) Act
1978	Inner Urban Areas Act
1980	Local Government Planning & Land Act

ENVIRONMENT

1953	Historic Buildings and Ancient Monuments Act
1953	Agricultural Land (Removal of Top Soil) Act
1958	Opencast Coal Act
1960	Caravan Sites and Control of Development Act
1960	Noise Abatement Act
1962	Local Authorities (Historic Buildings) Act
1962	Pipelines Act (and 1975)
1963	Agriculture Act
1963	Water Resources Act (and 1968)
1966	Commons Registration Act
1966	Mines (Working Facilities and Support) Act
1967	Forestry Act
1967	Civic Amenities Act
1968	Clean Air Act
1969	Redundant Churches Act
1970	Trees Act
1972	Local Government Act
1974	Control of Pollution Act
1974	Town & Country Planning (Amenities) Act
1978	Defence Disposal (Amenities) Act
1979	Ancient Monuments and Archaelogical Areas Act
1981	Wildlife and Countryside Act
1982	Town & Country Planning (Minerals) Act

TRANSPORT

1947	Transport Act (and 1953, 1962, 1968, 1978, 1980, 1983)
1959	Highways Act (and 1971, 1980)
1960	Road Traffic Act (and 1962)

LAND USE

HOUSING

1957	Housing Act (and 1961, 1964, 1974, 1975)
1967	Housing Subsidies Act
1972	Housing Finance Act
1980	Housing Act

EMPLOYMENT

1945	Distribution of Industry Act (and 1950, 1958)
1965	Control of Office and Industrial Development Act
1960	Local Employment Act (and 1970, 1972)
1966	Industrial Development Act
1969	Development of Tourism Act
1972	Industry Act (and 1975)

among the various civil service departments involved, and beyond them to all the multitude of interested parties. The organs of power, therefore, are more diffuse than may be suggested by our brief discussion here, and even while the legislation and structure may remain much the same, policy emphases are subject to influence and to change, according to the political preferences of particular governments and their response to changing events.

Department of the Environment

As an activity of local government, a major section of planning falls within the responsibilities of the DOE. As with any large, multi-function organisation, the Department is divided into several units and chains of command. These are susceptible to re-arrangement from time to time, but the organisation as at August 1984 is illustrated in Fig 1.2. The complexity of the system is such that political co-ordination is not easy, and criticism has been levelled at the Secretary of State for failing to draw together the activities of his junior ministers, who inevitably have to be allowed considerable freedom. By its nature, much of politics is reactive rather than creative, so ministers often find themselves taken up full time with one particular problem or another, to the detriment of their wider responsibilities. In such a way, Secretary of State Heseltine found himself devoting one day each week to the affairs of Merseyside for over a year after the riots in Toxteth in August 1981. Such trouble-shooting inevitably leaves the detailed formation of policy and its application in the hands of officials. Thus while ministers may find themselves preoccupied with particular policies, their officials, drawn from the various branches of the department may themselves wish to secure policies appropriate to their responsibilities, and in such ways it becomes particularly difficult to secure the all-round view of particular problems that it was hoped the creation of this large department would engender.

Figure 1.2   Organisation of the Department of the Environment

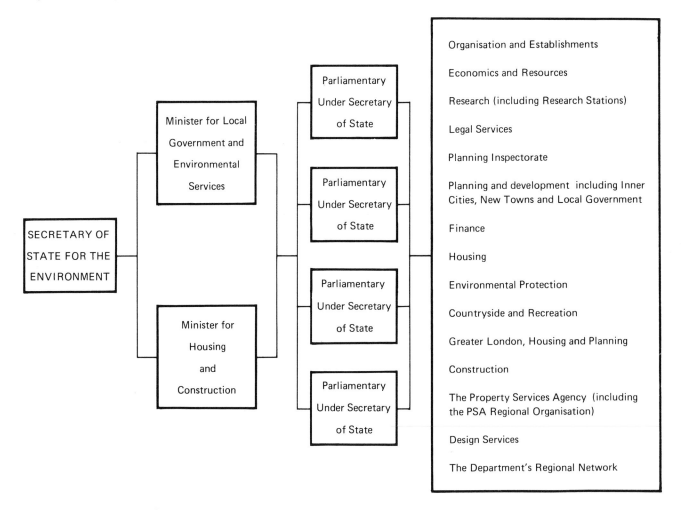

In addition to the central operation of the Department in London, the DOE also has a regional organisation which it shares with the Department of Transport. A permanent under secretary acts as Director at each of the eight regional offices which deal with matters relating to housing, land use planning, some transport issues and such regional planning as is now undertaken. The Department's officials are also, of course, involved in the work of a number of international organisations, most importantly, committees of the EEC.

Department of Transport

Although the Department of Transport formed part of the DOE between 1970–76, the importance of its work persuaded government that it should regain its independence. As with the DOE, not all of the DTp's functions bear directly upon planning. Its regulation of private transport, and its supervision of the nationalised transport industries are of consequence, but not of such material impact as the building and maintenance of motorways and trunk roads, and the allocation of funds to county councils in England for transport purposes. This latter is of fundamental importance.

Local transport planning is the responsibility of the county councils, but central supervision and grant allocation are the responsibility of the DTp through the system of *Transport Policies and Programmes (TPPs)* and the *Transport Supplementary Grant* (see Chapter 6). The intention of the system is that the various local authorities should prepare policies to respond locally to their specific needs in a comprehensive and integrated way. While this may encourage local autonomy, the real test is how much of its policy a local authority can actually put into effect, and that largely depends upon the level of support that is forthcoming in the way of Transport Supplementary Grant. This is decided annually by the Secretary of State on the basis of the TPP submitted by each county in the form of a five year rolling plan. This clearly enables central government to keep a very close watch not only upon the evolution of local policy, but in large measure to direct it and monitor its detailed application. Only in rare cases is there sufficient local political will to over-ride central policy and to bear the financial burdens of disapproval, as has been the case with the independent-minded South Yorkshire County Council.

Complementary to local transport planning is the need for a well-planned and maintained national road system. The building of motorways and trunk roads are major planning issues which affect not only the localities involved, but also the strategic planning of those counties through which such routes lie. Final decisions on all trunk road planning are taken jointly between the DOE and the DTp, but in the actual construction of roads, the DTp's staff directly inter-mesh with those of the county councils, who act as agents for the Department on smaller road schemes. Because of the local significance of these planning decisions, the Department has to provide for a proper system of public consultation, for public inquiries and appeals. This inspectorate service is shared with the DOE, but whereas the service can at least have the aspect of neutrality in the case of local planning matters, whose instigation lies with the local planning authority or a planning appellant, in the transport field, the inspectorate can all too easily appear to be judging their own cause, for the proposal also emanates from the same department.

The Scottish and Welsh Offices

Largely in response to Nationalist pressure, Secretaries of State for Scotland and Wales preside over multi-function offices which carry out, for their respective areas, most of the functions described above for England. In Scotland, the success of the Scottish National Party in the elections of 1926 and 1931 encouraged the government to establish a 'mini-Whitehall' at St. Andrew's House in Edinburgh. The responsibilities of the Scottish Office have been regularly added to, in what now amounts to a considerable degree of administrative devolution though under the control of a Cabinet Minister. In 1962 the *Scottish Development Department* was set up with wide-ranging powers of positive planning relating to housing, transport, industrial facilities and other developments. Unlike the DOE, the Scottish Office has introduced *national planning guidelines* to achieve nationally coherent local planning policies. Administrative devolution in Wales does not have such a long history, and it was only in 1964 that a Welsh Office was created, with very much slimmer responsibilities than its counterpart in Edinburgh. Unique to Wales, however, is the *Land Authority for Wales*, first constituted under the Community Land Act 1975. Under the Local Government, Planning and Land Act 1980, the Authority was maintained to acquire land for future development purposes. The Authority is appointed by the Secretary of State for Wales, and of its 6–9 members, at least four must be representative of the Welsh local authorities.

Other Ministries

In addition to the departments specifically responsible for planning matters, it is important to remember that the activities of other government departments bear heavily upon the planning function. Through its development of regional and other policies for industry and employment the *Department of Trade and Industry* has a significant impact upon the opportunities for local planning initiatives. In particular, the re-drawing of the map of regional aid in 1979 caused many local planning authorities to re-consider their own strategies. Acting within the provisions of the EEC's Common Agricultural Policy, the *Ministry of Agriculture, Fisheries and Food* has a major impact upon rural planning. Special provisions for hill and upland farming, for instance, are vital for the maintenance of many remote rural communities. Conservation in the countryside is of growing interest, and policies relating to the reclamation of marginal lands have recently provoked controversy for moorland and wetland conservation interests, while the preservation of historic landscapes along with access to archaeological sites bears directly upon agricultural practice. The pattern of crop subsidisation not only affects the visual appearance of the countryside, but has implications for the whole realm of farming practice, and the structure of local communities. Lastly, the operations of the *Ministry of Defence*, which lie outside the normal provision of planning controls, are locally significant not only for the reservation of training grounds, but also for the size and location of particular service bases. The relative fortunes of service bases, whether in well-established cities or remote rural areas, can pose considerable problems for the local planning authorities. Although such bases are often self-contained, their economic impact on the local community can be considerable in terms of civilian job opportunities, transport, and indirectly via the multiplier effect. Lastly, the Department of Energy through its policies and investment plans for the nationalised energy boards may have considerable impact, whether on the choice and siting of a nuclear power station, or the development of new coal or oil reserves.

Fringe Bodies

From time to time, governments have established a variety of ad hoc groups charged with undertaking specific tasks, or supervising the operation of particular functions. The term *Quasi-autonomous non/national governmental organisation* (*quango*) has been attached to these fringe bodies, a number of which have operated in the planning field. The majority of these bodies only have an advisory and promotional role, and answer to an appropriate government minister through an Annual Report. Nevertheless, in the formulation of policy they can have a significant impact, not always to the pleasure of the major government departments. Because such bodies are charged with a specific, and therefore a sectional interest, their advice is more partisan than policy which springs from a Department of State, which may be more broadly based. A good example of such a situation is the Countryside Commission, one of the major fringe bodies to survive the recent reduction in their numbers, and which has occasionally appeared against the DOE and the DTp at public inquiries. Despite Conservative antipathy towards fringe bodies, the concept is admitted to be useful, and in 1984 an important new fringe body was established in the Historic Buildings and Monuments Commission to undertake national responsibilities for scheduled ancient monuments (see Chapter 8).

1.2   CONTROL AT WORK

Direct Operations

By statute, central government has a direct involvement in planning matters, as well as a supervisory role over the activities of the local planning authorities. Such specific activity is most appropriately illustrated from the work of the DOE, carried out in the name of the Secretary of State. Thus the Department is responsible for the creation of special development initiatives. In the past this took the form of the designation of new towns, including the designation of land for development, the setting up of the Development Corporation and the provision of funds. Since 1979 such powers have been extended to include the designation of Urban Development Corporations within existing urban areas, as in the London Docklands and on Merseyside, and the establishment of Enterprise Zones (see Chapter 4). While local authorities are able to initiate proposals for such features, power to establish them remains firmly in the hands of the Department.

At a more local scale of operation, quite detailed applications of central policy emanate from the work of the *Property Services Agency* which is responsible not only for the design construction and letting of every crown building but also its furnishing. As the sovereign authority, the crown does not have to submit to the normal processes of development control outlined in Chapter 2, although usual practice is to make reference to it.

The regional organisation of the DOE and the DTp has already been noted, but in addition, most central departments have representatives on the *Regional Economic Planning Boards*, whose task is to co-ordinate the work of the departments in the English regions. While the regional co-ordination of departmental policies goes back to the exigencies of the 1939–45 war, central departments have rarely shown enthusiasm for the regional dimension. In part this is an inevitable consequence of the very existence of central departments to which non-central activities must appear subsidiary. Such a perspective is reinforced by a career structure whose top line of command has to be centrally based. Although the Regional Offices and the Regional Boards are a means by which central departments can be kept informed as to the needs and attitudes of the country at large, they are not there primarily to articulate a regional voice, but to ensure the effective discharge of central policies.

Supervisory Operations

i) Circulars Government legislation inevitably requires interpretation as it is applied in changing circumstances and to specific issues. In addition, much legislation specifically allows for quite wide powers of ministerial direction. Consequently it is necessary for central departments to issue circulars from time to time advising of new procedures or changes of emphasis or actual policy under an act. Such regulations may arise as a result of particular case experience, or as a result of changed financial provision, or a modification of policy consequent upon political changes. A major difficulty with this means of communication is that the degree of compulsion within the circulars is often ambiguous, and the response of local authorities may well depend upon their political outlook as much as to the circumstances which have given rise to a particular circular. An interesting point of difference between England and Scotland is the provision by the Scottish Office of 'national planning guidelines', introduced in 1977 and revised in 1981. These make much more explicit than is the case in England and Wales, the areas of planning in which central government wishes to take a special role, and they form the basis of a national planning policy.

ii) Approval of statutory plans This is the most formal aspect of central supervision. Central activity is not limited simply to the approval of plans, or to requirements to make modifications to submitted plans, for as will be seen in Chapter 2, officials from central departments are involved in a consultative and monitoring ca-

pacity during the preparation of, for instance, Structure Plans. Reference has already been made to the development of Transport Policies and Programmes which require ministerial approval. In a similar way, local authorities also have to produce *Housing Investment Programmes* on a four year rolling basis to cover their intentions as regards council housing, grants to the private sector and the support of housing associations (see Chapter 3). The role of central government in development control is discussed in Chapter 2, but for completeness we can note here that the operation of the planning inspectorate plays a part in the evolution of case law. Unfortunately inconsistencies can arise between various inspectors in related applications, and also in the view of the Minister, who may well over-rule an inspector's recommendation. Thus in 1984 the Secretary of State approved a multi-million pound housing and office scheme for the Free Trade Wharf site in the London borough of Tower Hamlets, in the face of his inspector's recommendation that the proposed development be turned down because it was so out of harmony with its surroundings as to be unacceptable.

iii) Financial controls Within the statutory abilities of local government, the size of a local authority's budget determines the scope of its operations. Although planning as such takes a very small part of the budget, the subjects of planning such as housing, transport infrastructure, redevelopment proposals, conservation activity etc., may form significant amounts of capital and recurrent expenditure. Expenditure for major capital projects will require loan sanction from central government, which is a means by which central government not only attempts to control the public sector borrowing requirement, but is also a mechanism by which the nature of capital projects can be supervised. Smaller capital projects, and the finance required for Housing Investment Programmes are contained within the provisions of the *block grant* made each year to individual local authorities, a feature which has proved increasingly contentious over the early 1980's.

Central government has been increasingly alarmed at its contribution to local government finances since 1975–6, when central grants averaged 66.5% of local government expenditure (the remainder being made up from the rates and from trading operations). After Defence, the block grants to local authorities have formed the most important item of central government expenditure. For a government determined to reduce public expenditure, local government support was an obvious target. Within the provisions of the 1980 Local Government, Planning and Land Act, the government took powers to re-arrange the method of calculating the block grant (to the disadvantage of the largest urban authorities), aimed to reduce the proportion of its contribution (reduced to 52% in 1984–5), and introduced penalties for what it determined to be excessive rate rises to cover budget deficits. In 1984 it also introduced powers to limit or 'cap' the level of rates to be levied in 1985, striking at local government's major independent source of funds, and hence, it is argued, at local democracy itself.

This significant degree of central control over local government finance is the key to the present relationship between central and local government and has overshadowed in recent years other aspects of financial control. These include audit control, which goes far beyond simply 'checking the books' and extends to ensuring that there is a proper legal justification for all expenditure. This prevents a local authority from embarking on illegal expenses and also allows a detailed scrutiny of an authority's work. Lastly, financial controls are also evident in the cost-yardstick approach. This requires local authorities to adhere to certain cost ceilings in the preparation of plans. The identification of cost yardsticks is part of the research function of central departments.

Local Government Responses

The degree of involvement of central government in the political realm of which planning is an integral aspect has been seriously questioned since the mid 1960's. More recently the Labour and both the Alliance parties have all expressed a commitment to some form of devolution of power from the centre. It must not be thought, however, that local government is itself unable to influence the centre. The reduction in the block grant has been vigorously fought. Although most local authorities have unwillingly acquiesced, the City of Liverpool District Council almost failed to construct a budget for 1984–5 in a successful attempt to force the government to give more financial support. This was an extreme position and could have involved local councillors in severe personal penalties. In more normal circumstances formal and informal lobbying is achieved through members of both Houses of Parliament and through the party networks, while local government officers and civil servants are in regular contact, facilitating the exchange of views. Representation at the highest levels, however, is made by way of the prestigious local authority associations (Association of County Councils, Association of District Councils and the Association of Metropolitan Authorities).

Further reading

For more detailed information on the DOE see *The DOE and its Work: a Factual Note about the Functions of the DOE* (DOE, 1979), and for a critique M J Painter 1980 Policy co-ordination in the DOE 1970–76 *Public Administration* 53, 135–154. A fascinating glimpse of the inner workings of central government was offered by Richard Crossman's diaries: see A Howard 1979 *The Crossman Diaries* (Magnum). Useful introductions to the problems of centre-local relationships will be found in R Hambleton 1978 *Policy Planning and Local Government* (Hutchinson) Chapter 1 and in G Cameron (ed) 1980 *The Future of the British Conurbations* (Longman) Chs 4 and 13. Part 1 of R Bennett (1982) *Central Grants to Local Government* (C.U.P.) gives an interesting analysis of the variation of central grants between the various local authorities.

CHAPTER 2
LOCAL GOVERNMENT AS THE PLANNING AUTHORITY

2.1   INTRODUCTION TO LOCAL GOVERNMENT

Structure

Local government operates as a set of autonomous authorities upon whom specific powers are conferred. District Councils are not a sub set of the County Councils in England and Wales, nor of the Regional Councils in Scotland, and neither are a sub set of central government. Parish and Community Councils, District Councils, Scottish Regional Councils and the English and Welsh County Councils are all composed of directly elected members, and have the ability to raise revenue for their specific purposes. The County, Regional and District Councils each have planning powers, and the Parish and Community Councils have the right to notify the planning authority that they wish to be consulted about all planning applications in their area (Fig 2.1).

The present structure of local government is the result of a series of reforms, beginning with that of Greater London in 1963. A Royal Commission on Local

Figure 2.1   Planning and Local Government

Structure Planning	Local Planning	Consultation only
LONDON Greater London Council	London Boroughs	
ENGLAND & WALES 42 County Councils (6 Metro)	332 District Councils (36 Metro)	Parish Councils
SCOTLAND 6 Regional Councils 3 General Planning Authorities for 16 Districts 3 Island General Planning Authorities	37 District Councils	Community Councils

Government in England (Redcliffe-Maud Commission) reported in 1969 and set the scene for re-organisation in England and Wales, with a parallel report (Wheatley Commission) for Scotland. In Scotland, a more radical restructuring was accepted which involved the creation of a series of unequal regions with varying powers and sometimes including a lower tier of districts. In England and Wales the restructure was more conservative. Although the Royal Commission proposed a unitary system largely based on existing counties, with the exception of three 'metropolitan' counties where a two-tier structure was proposed (in the West Midlands, Greater Manchester and Merseyside), the 1972 Local Government Act implemented a two tier system of counties and districts. Additional metropolitan counties were also created in West and South Yorkshire and in Tyne and Wear. The major difference between the metropolitan and the 'shire' counties was that responsibility for education, libraries and the social services was given to the districts rather than to the counties, leaving the metropolitan counties with relatively few functions relating to the emergency services, strategic transport and road functions, structure planning, refuse disposal and discretionary powers in the field of arts and recreation. This rather limited role led to the Conservative proposals in 1983 to abolish the metropolitan counties, and the Greater London Council on which they were largely modelled, as an unnecessary and wasteful tier of government whose functions could be adequately discharged at a lower level by the districts (and London Boroughs) acting either individually, or co-operatively, through a system of indirectly elected joint boards, or by agency agreements (one district taking on county-wide responsibilities on behalf of the others). These proposals neatly turned the Redcliffe Maud Commission on its head by substituting a unitary system where the Commission proposed two tiers and leaving two tiers where it preferred one!

From a planning point of view, there is no doubt that a system of unitary authorities based upon travel to work areas would have been generally preferred for England and Wales. This was indeed presumed by the 1968 Town and Country Planning Act (1969 for Scotland) which re-organised the planning function into *structure* and *local* planning. In the event, only a small proportion of English districts contain complete travel to work areas (generally with populations of less than 60–70,000) and some districts still appear as urban 'islands' surrounded by another 'rural' district. Outside the metropolitan areas some large cities (with the reduced status of districts within counties) still exert considerable influence not only over neighbouring districts in the same county, but in cases such as Bristol and Plymouth over whole neighbouring counties. The major issue in the metropolitan areas is now the degree to which structure planning can be successfully undertaken on the removal of the county council. It must be admitted that since the completion of the county structure plans, most county planning teams are only a fraction of their former size, but it seems doubtful that the individual districts, even with the benefit of central supervision and local consultation will be able to undertake the task as coherently or disinterestedly.

Operation

As in national government, local government is conducted by a dual system of elected members (the councillors) and remunerated employees (local government officers). The operation of the system thus depends upon the successful interaction of these two groups within themselves, between each other, and with the general public as electors and as the receivers of the various services that are discharged (Fig 2.2). This inevitably introduces a social as well as a political dimension into what on the surface might appear to be a very formalised bureaucratic machine.

i) Elected members   When reference is made to a *local authority* this means the elected members who make up the council concerned, although in practice the day to day exercise of the responsibilities of the local authority is in the hands of the officers. Nevertheless, the principle of public accountability requires that officers should answer to councillors, who are in turn obliged to submit themselves to the electorate at four-yearly intervals. Some councillors are mainly interested in looking after the interests of their own ward and electorate, almost to the point of acting as unpaid social workers, while others have a greater enthusiasm for policy-making. Some are pragmatic in approach, while others are deeply committed to a political ideology. Some council members, even though members of a political party often act independently of party policy, while others are happy to follow the party line. All of these attributes come together in varying degrees along with the force of individual personalities and the weight of experience. Thus the decision making process is very subtle, and by no means the mechanical event which might be supposed.

While many members of the public aver that 'politics should be kept out of local government', political partisanship has increased in recent years with more West-

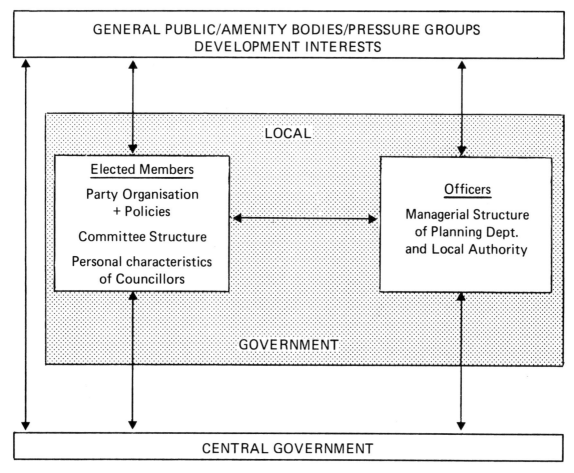

Figure 2.2   Parties in the Planning Process

minster style block voting not only in full council but also in committees. This means that many matters are effectively settled in party group meetings outside the formal committee structure. Where a particular party has a strong majority, the policy-making strength of the minority groups is thus virtually eclipsed, although councillors are still able to function as advocates for aggrieved constituents. Nevertheless, political parties have an important role to play in articulating alternative policy options, mobilising electoral support and through the national organisation, providing useful background research and advice.

ii) Officers and management structure The elected member can rarely be involved with the technical and detailed aspects of policy generation and application, which must be left to officers. The interface between officers and elected members, however, occurs via the overall management structure adopted by the local authority and its attendant committee structure. This latter may be extremely complex and involve a ramifying network of sub committees and working parties be-

neath the major committees. The committees and their constituent sets are the real workshops of the local authority, and are the means by which officers advise elected members and through them the local authority itself. Although local authorities are in theory free to devise their own structures of management and policy making, two major influences have contributed to a certain similarity between authorities. The first is the statutory requirement upon local authorities to have certain committees, e.g. as planning authorities, both county and district councils must have planning committees, just as an education committee is a requirement of county councils and metropolitan district councils, since they are the local education authority. The second is the impact of the Bains Report (1972) upon the newly constituted local authorities. The Bains Committee was appointed jointly by the Secretary of State for the Environment and the local authority associations. In its report proposals were made as to the type of management structure which would be appropriate for the new local authorities taking office in 1974. The report was strongly influenced by a variety of new approaches to management which had been circulating in both the private and the public sector for the previous ten or fifteen years. These emphasised the need for what was termed 'corporate' approaches to management and planning, enabling institutional structures to be goal or problem oriented. As these approaches were applied to local government, the Bains Report made three principal innovations

- the appointment of a Chief Executive who would act as chief adviser in executive terms
- the creation of a Policy and Resources committee of elected members to provide advice on policy priorities
- the establishment of a management team of principal officers whose job would be to co-ordinate the various activities of the council in accordance with the council's policies.

Almost all the new authorities followed this pattern, which together with the requirement for the statutory committees gave little room for variation in overall structure.

Following a goal-oriented or problem-solving approach means that planning in its widest sense becomes a feature of each of the local authority departments – social services, housing, education, leisure services etc. as they each work through a programme of action towards their identified goals. Because of its holistic and forward-looking nature, however, town and country planning itself can have a key role in such an approach since it can be a means of resolving on the ground the various needs of a particular authority. Thus, particularly at county level the structure planning process has sometimes been the means by which a 'corporate plan' has been devised. In the event, not as much has been achieved by this new approach as was envisaged. The identification of realistic objectives, for instance, has been very difficult. The 'elimination of deprivation' or the 'promotion of well-being' are much more elusive concepts than the achievement by a private company of a certain level of turnover. In this sense, the local authority is not like a business, and balance sheet techniques are therefore inappropriate. In the event, too, economic recession has made growth-oriented strategies, indeed any strategic thinking, very difficult to achieve, particularly insofar as local authorities have only limited freedom of action in relation to the private enterprises within their area, as will be seen particularly in Chapter 4.

2.2 STRUCTURE PLANNING

Aims and Objectives

Under the 1968 Town and Country Planning Act (1969 for Scotland), now consolidated in the 1971 Act (1972 for Scotland), County Councils in England and Wales, and Regional Councils in Scotland are required to produce a *Structure Plan* setting out the 'local authority's policy and general proposals in respect of the development and other use of land in that area'. In doing so the plan must have due regard to national and regional policy and take account of the strategies of neighbouring authorities. The Structure Plan is concerned with establishing long term strategy for the county or region, and provides the framework and statutory basis for local plans. Some elements of the plan may refer to a twenty–thirty year time scale, whilst others may be more immediate. Irrespective of timescale involved, the plan can never be completed finally as evaluation and monitoring of the plan and its progress is intended to be continuous, so that it can be adapted to meet changing requirements.

A Structure Plan identifies certain broad aims, or general statements of intent and then specifies particular objectives by which it is hoped these aims will be achieved. One of the plan's roles is to identify the alternative courses of action which may be undertaken, and Table 2, taken from the Dyfed Structure Plan, illustrates the range of options seen as available in realising the intentions of the plan.

Format and Procedure

The specific content of each structure plan will obviously vary considerably between areas, but both format and procedure are the subject of statute, supplemented by circulars and advice from the DOE. Thus, during the 1970's several circulars were issued which had the effect of limiting coverage within the plan to key areas requiring the most urgent attention. The Act requires that all development plans be based on a survey 'examining the matters which may be expected to affect the development of that area or the planning of its development'. Typically, these matters include the physical, economic, demographic and transport characteristics of the area. The results of these analyses are compiled into a *Report of Survey* which ultimately forms part of a suite of structure plan documents. In this way it is possible to identify issues relating to particular topics, and also to specific

SUBJECT	ISSUE	OBJECTIVE	FEASIBLE OPTIONS
EMPLOYMENT	The most appropriate locations for the development of future employment.	1) To encourage an adequate range of employment opportunities in the County 2) To ensure the provision of an adequate supply of land and suitable range of sites for industrial and commercial development.	**LOCATION OF EMPLOYMENT** (i) **Limited Concentration** This would give emphasis to a limited number of selected main towns which could accommodate employment growth. Major developments would be steered towards the Aberystwyth, Llanelli and Milford Haven Waterway areas. (ii) **DISPERSAL** WHILST EMPHASIS FOR MAJOR DEVELOPMENTS IS STILL PLACED WITHIN THE ABERYSTWYTH, LLANELLI AND MILFORD HAVEN WATERWAY AREAS, ADDITIONAL EMPLOYMENT OPPORTUNITIES WOULD BE ENCOURAGED IN A WIDE VARIETY OF SMALLER CENTRES WHERE EMPLOYMENT GROWTH COULD BE ACCOMMODATED.
HOUSING	The most appropriate locations for the development of housing.	1) To ensure that provision is made on a continuing basis for adequate numbers and choice of houses sufficient to meet the needs of the areas, expected population. 2) To ensure that the location of residential development is related to work, shops, leisure and community facilities	**LOCATION OF HOUSING** (i) **Limited Concentration** This would entail most residential development taking place within the main towns and associated settlements in close proximity. (ii) **DISPERSAL** THIS INVOLVES A GREATER EMPHASIS BEING PLACED UPON SPREADING HOUSING DEVELOPMENT NOT ONLY INTO THE MAIN TOWNS AND ASSOCIATED SETTLEMENTS BUT ALSO INTO A WIDE RANGE OF SMALLER SETTLEMENTS IN THE COUNTY.
TRANSPORT	a) The most appropriate locations for transportation investment in relation to the existing and future location and scale of housing, employment, tourism Celtic Sea Oil and other activities. b) The priority attached to different means of transport (public and private).	To promote the development of an efficient transport system to meet the needs of the County	**LOCATION OF TRANSPORT INVESTMENT** (i) **Limited Concentration** Resources would be concentrated on routes within and between the main urban areas of the County. (ii) **DISPERSAL** A MORE WIDESPREAD DISTRIBUTION OF INVESTMENT ON BOTH MAJOR AND MINOR ROADS THROUGHOUT THE COUNTY **PRIORITY OF PUBLIC TRANSPORT** (i) **Reduction** Full emphasis would be placed upon the provision of private transport facilities with limited priority being given to the public transport system. (ii) **Maintenance** Moderate investment in private transport facilities would take place allied to the maintenance of the existing level of public transport provision. (iii) **INCREASE** PROVISION OF IMPROVED PUBLIC TRANSPORT
TOURISM	a) The most appropriate locations for any further tourist related developments b) The scale of tourism development that can be acceptably accommodated in Dyfed including the types of development that should be encouraged or discouraged	To ensure an adequate level of provision of tourist facilities in the County.	**LOCATION OF TOURIST ACCOMMODATION** (i) **Concentration** This would involve the development of tourist accommodation at a limited number of major tourist centres. (ii) **LIMITED CONCENTRATION** THIS WOULD AIM TO SPREAD TOURIST ACCOMMODATION DEVELOPMENTS INTO A WIDE RANGE OF APPROPRIATE CENTRES BUT NOT INTO OPEN COUNTRYSIDE UNRELATED TO EXISTING SETTLEMENTS. (iii) **Dispersal** There would be no general presumption against the development of tourist accommodation in open countryside unrelated to existing settlements. **SCALE OF TOURIST ACCOMMODATION** (i) **Expansion** An overall increase in the level of tourist accommodation with the exception that static caravans and chalets in the coastal areas would be generally resisted. (ii) **MAINTENANCE** INVOLVES KEEPING THE LEVEL OF ACCOMMODATION BROADLY AS AT PRESENT THOUGH CHANGES BETWEEN SECTORS OF THE INDUSTRY WOULD BE POSSIBLE; STRICT CONTROL OVER FURTHER CARAVANS AND CHALETS AND EMPHASIS ON THOSE FORMS OF ACCOMMODATION MOST BENEFICIAL TO THE COUNTY. (iii) **Discouragement** A reduction in the overall provision of accommodation although increases in certain sectors possible. General presumption against further caravan and chalet development over the County and reductions made in the existing level of provision wherever possible.

Continued Overleaf

Table 2   Dyfed C.C. Structure Planning: issues, objectives and options

-2-

SUBJECT	ISSUE	OBJECTIVE	FEASIBLE OPTIONS
RECREATION	The appropriate location, scale and type of recreation facilities.	To ensure an adequate level of recreation provision to meet both local and national needs.	**SCALE OF RECREATION FACILITIES** (i) **ENCOURAGEMENT** MORE FACILITIES FOR RECREATION WOULD BE PROVIDED BY THE COUNTY COUNCIL AND OTHER AGENCIES. (ii) **Maintenance** The general current level of provision would be maintained but no major expansion of facilities by the County Council would be involved.
MAJOR OIL AND GAS DEVELOPMENTS	a) The most appropriate locations for any further oil and gas related developments. b) The scale of oil and gas development that can be acceptably accommodated in Dyfed including the types of development that should be encouraged or discouraged.	To ensure that adequate provision is made for the development of oil and gas related facilities in the County.	**LOCATION OF MAJOR OIL AND GAS DEVELOPMENTS** (i) **CONCENTRATION** THIS WOULD INVOLVE THE CONCENTRATION OF ALL APPROPRIATE DEVELOPMENTS WITHIN THE MILFORD HAVEN WATERWAY AREA. (ii) **Limited Concentration** Appropriate developments would be located within the Aberystwyth, Llanelli and Milford Haven Waterway areas. **SCALE OF MAJOR OIL AND GAS DEVELOPMENTS** (i) **Encouragement** Those forms of major oil and gas developments which were technically feasible in Dyfed would be encouraged. (ii) **SELECTIVE ENCOURAGEMENT** THIS WOULD INVOLVE THE EXCLUSION OF THOSE TYPES OF DEVELOPMENT WITH FAR REACHING ADVERSE ENVIRONMENTAL EFFECTS. (iii) **Discouragement** Only those types of major oil and gas development which could be clearly seen to have no significant environmental conflicts and have long term economic benefits to the County would be acceptable.
MINERAL DEVELOPMENT	The scale of mineral working that can be acceptably accommodated in Dyfed.	To ensure that adequate provision is made for the conservation and development of mineral resources in Dyfed.	**SCALE OF MINERAL DEVELOPMENT** (i) **Encouragement** Those forms of mineral development which were considered to be technically feasible would be encouraged. (ii) **SELECTIVE ENCOURAGEMENT** MINERAL DEVELOPMENTS LIKELY TO RESULT IN A HIGH LEVEL OF ENVIRONMENTAL IMPACT WOULD BE RESISTED.
URBAN AND RURAL ENVIRONMENT	The degree of consideration and protection which should be given to agriculture, forestry and the environment, including in particular the conservation of ecological, visual historical and archaeological factors both urban and rural.	To protect and enhance the environment as far as practicable. To encourage the full utilisation of agriculture and forestry in Dyfed.	**CONSERVATION OF URBAN ENVIRONMENT** (i) **High Emphasis** Maximum priority would be afforded to the conservation of the urban resources of the County. (ii) **MEDIUM EMPHASIS** PRIORITY WOULD BE GIVEN TO URBAN FEATURES OF GREATEST SIGNIFICANCE WITH A LESS RESTRICTIVE ATTITUDE ELSEWHERE. **CONSERVATION OF RURAL ENVIRONMENT** (i) **High Emphasis** Maximum priority afforded to the conservation of high quality rural environment. (ii) **MEDIUM EMPHASIS** PRIORITY WOULD BE GIVEN TO NATURAL ENVIRONMENT AREAS OF THE GREATEST SIGNIFICANCE WITH A LESS RESTRICTIVE ATTITUDE BEING APPLIED OUTSIDE THESE AREAS, EXCEPT IN THE PEMBROKESHIRE COAST NATIONAL PARK AND BRECON BEACONS NATIONAL PARK WHERE HIGH EMPHASIS APPLIES.

Source: Dyfed County Council
Structure Plan, March 1980

areas of the county. Subjects seen as appropriate for treatment by a structure plan include:

Population	Employment	Resources
Housing	Industry	Commerce
Minerals	Transport	Shopping
Education	Conservation	Social Services
Public Utilities	Leisure and Recreation	

Having identified the main issues and problems in the context of established aims and objectives, the county then has to formulate alternative strategies that could be pursued. These are often based on different growth rate assumptions, and are then evaluated against each other in order to discern which combination would best secure the long term interests of the county (Fig 2.3). Throughout the formative stages of a structure plan, including the survey, the local planning authority must

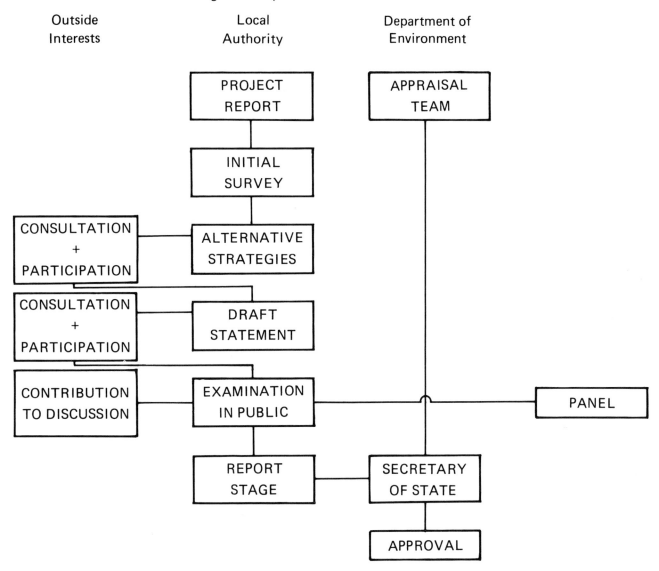

Figure 2.3   Stages in Structure Plan preparation

ensure that adequate publicity is given to their activities and intentions. They must also consider which people or group of people might wish to comment, and ensure that they are made aware of their right, and given adequate time to do so. Public opinion is then incorporated in the technical evaluation of alternatives in the light of such practical constraints as are apparent.

Priorities established, a Draft Plan is composed when further public comment is sought. After appropriate amendments have been made the plan is finally submitted to the Secretary of State. At this point it should be noted that the DOE has already had a small team of its own officials monitoring the progress and content of the plan preparation. The Structure Plan presented consists of a *written statement* describing the local planning auth-

ority's policy and general proposals, accompanied by a reasoned justification and appropriately illustrated in diagrammatic form. The illustrations should include a *key diagram* showing the general nature of the policies and proposals in broad terms (Fig 2.4). Although matters relating to specific sites and therefore requiring a map base are a function of local planning, the structure plan may designate *action areas* for which a detailed plan must be produced. Finally the authority must indicate that they have complied with the public participation procedures laid down by the 1971 Act before the Minister will proceed to consider the plan.

At the same time as the plan is submitted to the Minister, copies must also be made available for inspection locally and time allowed for objections to be made to

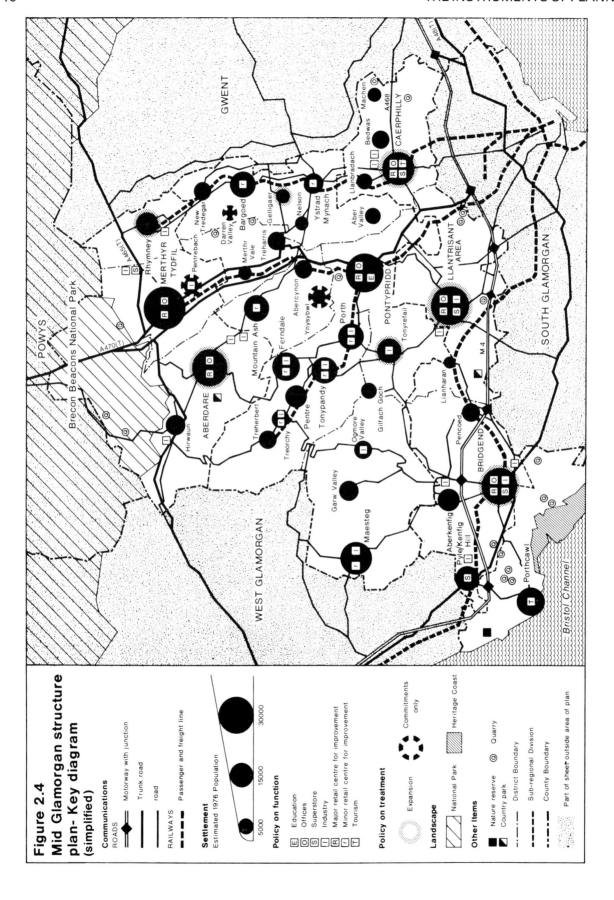

Figure 2.4
Mid Glamorgan structure plan- Key diagram (simplified)

Communications

ROADS

◆ Motorway with junction

Trunk road

road

RAILWAYS

Passenger and freight line

Settlement

Estimated 1976 Population

5000   15000   30000

Policy on function

E Education
O Offices
S Superstore
I Industry
R Major retail centre for improvement
r Minor retail centre for improvement
T Tourism

Policy on treatment

Expansion

Commitments only

Landscape

National Park

Heritage Coast

Other items

■ Nature reserve
■ Country park
◎ Quarry
District Boundary
Sub-regional Division
County Boundary
Part of sheet outside area of plan

the Minister, who will then consider such objections as are made. The Minister is empowered to hold an *examination in public* of any matters he feels merit a public hearing. Technically, no objector has the statutory right to be heard at an examination in public, not even the planning authority whose plan is being scrutinised, although, of course, their absence would obviously hinder proper examination. The contentious issues are heard and considered over a period of several weeks by an impartial panel who report to the Secretary of State. The plan may then be approved with or without modifications, but if any modifications are made, public notice must be given and any further objections heard before the Secretary of State will give his final approval.

Appraisal

i) Scope and content A Structure Plan is an approach to a problem rather than a strictly itemised recipe for success. As such it is not surprising that submitted plans should vary so much in scope and content, yet this of itself has provoked considerable discussion as planning teams in various parts of the country have sought to apply the approach to their own circumstances. In so far as the process has been seen as a 'corporate planning' exercise there has been considerable dissension over the extent to which planners should get involved in matters over which they have no competence or influence, rather than keep strictly to matters of physical land use planning. On the other hand it is argued that such matters cannot be divorced from their socio-economic context. DOE response to the variety of the plans submitted has been ambivalent, on the one hand emphasising the need for a broad awareness of the physical, social and economic trends affecting a county, yet on the other criticising some plans for covering ground beyond that which is felt to be appropriate. In this respect the Scottish experience appears to be more successful, allowing greater flexibility in the Regional Reports which enables them to be used more clearly as corporate plans.

ii) Methodology While the policies themselves and the ways in which they are formulated are closely tied to local circumstances, it is possible to identify a certain unity of general practice which owes much to trends in decision-making theory since the 1960's. The structure planning process, as conceived in the 1968 Act was seen as a rational sequence of events passing through stages of aim generation, formulation of alternative strategies and selection of a preferred option, but as already noted in Section 2.1, the identification of appropriate and

meaningful aims has proved extremely elusive. By the early 1970's, planners were beginning to question the validity of this aims based methodology. The necessity of achieving a consensus of aims meant that those that could be agreed upon were often superficial, unrelated to the survey upon which they were supposedly based and very difficult to relate to specific policy measures.

For many planners, frustrated with the 'aims' approach, a problem oriented methodology seemed an appropriate alternative. The same decision making process could be followed, except that strategies could be based on surveyed *problems* rather than abstract aims. Alternative policies could then be evaluated, not by reference to abstract targets, but according to financial resources, political desirability and general practicability.

During the 1970's, planners also looked towards the alternative models of incrementalism and mixed scanning. The *incrementalist* approach is also problem oriented, but lacks the 'rational' overview as it is simply a response to problems as they arise. Incrementalism does not imply any major change in attitudes or structures and is usually much more politically acceptable. Unfortunately, since it is implicit and subjective, any vision that planners may hold of the future is inevitably hidden from the public with this approach.

Mixed scanning is effectively a compromise in the interests of pragmatism, since it combines elements of both the rational and incremental approaches. It recognises the need for some long term wider policy framework, usually of the less ambitious kind mentioned earlier, as well as more immediate treatment of key issues. Most counties have effectively operated a mixed scanning basis even though it may not have been a conscious choice, rather being influenced by DOE instructions to focus on key issues.

A popular argument is that there is little difference between the 'aims' and 'problems' approaches, since to identify a problem and design policies to alleviate it implies aims of some kind. On the other hand, aim relates to some future desired condition, maybe very different from present circumstances, while a problem reflects an existing situation. To base policy on the latter may be tantamount to acceptance of the status quo – which is effectively what most counties have done by opting for a problem approach within a mixed scanning framework. This pragmatic approach has led to a large number of structure plan policies revolving around issues which require short term solutions (such as allocating land for industry and housing, improving the road network, or providing recreational facilities) rather than being based on some social ideal which is unattainable at county level given the current range of planning control. While it may be impossible to get politicians to agree on social ideals, they can more readily accept that certain problems exist and require solution. Equally, it is easy to agree that structure plan policies should 'promote social well-being' and 'maintain and improve environmental quality', but there is less consensus for the more radical hopes that some have had for structure planning.

iii) Techniques Because of the strategic nature of structure planning there has been a need for effective forecasting techniques to identify the nature and direction of changes within a county, and to assess the possible impact of particular policy options. A range of technical devices have been used to establish trends and patterns in the interaction of demographic structure, employment opportunities, the provision of housing and education, recreation and transport facilities etc. Particular techniques used have varied enormously but most analyses by structure plan authorities are united by their similar frames of reference. The need for structure plan policies to be strategic in nature has meant that all authorities have had to pay some attention to *forecasts* of future needs and requirements. Usually it is only issues of 'key structural importance' – population, housing, employment and transport – that have been considered, and in most cases the forecasts performed have been of the orthodox type consisting of an extrapolation of existing trends, possibly weighted in some way. Usually forecasts have been made for a particular primary activity to provide the basis for estimates of supposedly dependent activities. Thus, population and activity rates have been used to provide the basis of labour supply estimates, or population and headship rates used to forecast household formation and consequent demand for housing, social services and education. This form of forecasting is attractive since it makes only limited demands on data and expertise, is relatively quick and responsive and is easily understood and explained to non-planners. Unfortunately such methods fail to accommodate the complexity of change among dynamic and inter-related activities, producing supply based estimates of population, labour supply, household formation etc. and not demand based requirements. Most forecasts have been projections rather than predictions - extrapolations of existing trends rather than policy-based views of the future. Predictions can arise from a consideration of alternative futures generated by these projections, but it seems that

most counties preferred not to take the process to this second stage. Perhaps understandably, it is those counties faced with the most severe problems that have considered the more sophisticated need or demand based approach, given that they are committed to avoiding a trend-based future.

In common with developments generally in the social sciences, planners have tended to move away from unbounded enthusiasm for strictly quantitative methods. Large scale modelling exercises particularly for shopping and land use/transportation requirements have varied in popularity because of the demands they make on data, time and staff expertise. Where quantitative techniques and modelling procedures are used, they tend now to be applied with much more selectivity and discrimination. The same applies to a range of techniques that have been used to evaluate alternative strategies in terms of their relative benefits. *Cost-benefit analysis* and the *planning balance sheet* attempt to achieve this objective by giving both the positive and negative impacts of a proposed development a monetary or numerical value, wherever possible. The *goals achievement matrix* recognises the difficulty of doing so and evaluates alternatives qualitatively on the basis of whether or not they achieve certain objectives, which in turn are weighted according to their priority, or perhaps their political appeal.

iv) Participation The lack of definition surrounding the scope of the structure plan has meant that it has been equally difficult to define the scope of public participation. In many cases, questions have been posed at a level which the public found difficult to relate to or to understand. There is popular confusion over county and district responsibilities for planning control, so consequently there has often been a mis-match between the intention behind the participation exercises and the response from the public. 'Participation' usually took the form of exhibitions both mobile and static, questionnaire surveys of opinion, meetings with organised groups, seminars with consultative committees and a limited amount of media exposure. In practice, few participate. In East Sussex, for instance, only between 1–2% became involved in the structure plan procedure between 1974–8. Such measures may thus be little more than a public information exercise and at best consultation, rather than true participation. It could be argued that all the statute requires is 'publicity' and the allowing of 'representations'. At the final stage it could be argued that the '*Examination in Public*' which has replaced the old '*Public Inquiry*' with its right to be heard, has reduced the opportunity for participation at the critical final stage.

The 1970's were undoubtedly a proving ground for participation methods and ideas. In the early years, the planning profession was breaking into an entirely new field with little custom and experience to guide it. To some extent, the legislation assumed a rational public, ready to express well-formulated opinions. In 1969 the *Skeffington Report* recognised that much more effort was required to involve the large numbers of habitual 'non-joiners'. Community education and planning aid by community development officers were suggested, for example, but none of this materialised, and requirements for this lively form of participation were never incorporated into subsequent legislation. Public participation quickly became institutionalised as a technical procedure which would ultimately legitimise the production of the final plan. The price to pay for this was the long delay involved which tended to slow down the speed at which the final plan was produced.

Clearly, a great deal has now been learned. There is general agreement that some form of participation is desirable, but that it is important to distinguish between continuous participation in the planning process and participation at set points in the production of a plan. While the district planning authority may consider the former in its production of local plans, it seems impractical to think of anything but the latter for the county planning authority engaged on a structure plan. It has, however, been suggested that once the plan has been produced, a form of continuous participation might be desirable as part of the monitoring process. This could be achieved through the creation of community forums, similar to the Scottish Community Councils set up in 1973. Equally, there is probably still a great deal of scope in utilising the existing system of elected members more effectively. It has been suggested that the whole act of public participation undermines the role of the elected member, although many councillors are often extremely busy, and have neither the time nor the inclination to closely examine the range of material produced in the structure planning process. On the other hand, close liaison between planner and councillor is very necessary, in that the former is prevented from viewing the area simply through maps, diagrams and statistics, and the latter is made aware of the wider implications of local authority policies.

v) Implementation Although County Council powers and responsibilities in the planning field have never been great, the financial and development control implications of the Local Government, Planning and Land Act, 1980, have left them with even fewer powers to implement their statutory policies. The Act confirms the strategic role of the county planners, but apart from a small number of exceptions all development control work is now carried out at district level. The districts must ensure that any development permitted conforms to the Structure Plan, and on matters of 'strategic importance' the county must be 'consulted'. Formerly counties were empowered to over-ride districts by 'calling-in' applications for strategic considerations. These powers were however removed by the Act (except for Highway matters). The extent to which structure plan policies are implemented, therefore, will depend very much on the relationships between county and district. Few are hostile and it seems doubtful whether many rogue decisions will be made that fundamentally undermine structure plan strategies now that the threat of county intervention has been removed. Since 1974 there have been remarkably few cases where counties have exercised their right of call-in, since most inconsistencies are sorted out informally. In fact there seems to be more cases of disputes between neighbouring counties, and with central government, than between counties and their districts, although notable exceptions have occurred. In Scotland, the Regions have retained their right of call-in on applications raising major planning issues, and are empowered to take enforcement action in cases where structure plan provisions are materially prejudiced.

vi) Monitoring Despite its loss of development control functions, the county still has a valuable monitoring role to perform in continuously evaluating and modifying structure plan policies. The scale of this role will obviously vary according to the size and complexity of a county and the range and scale of problems it faces. The process has begun to yield brief annual monitoring documents covering national and regional trends, and developments in the county on a topic by topic basis, e.g. socio-economic variables, land use change, changes in government policy applications, along with how the county strategy has been affected. The DOE has felt the need to advise local planning authorities on the need for precision and clarity when these policy statements are formulated, so that they identify the principal current issues in such a way as to encourage discussion and consultation, and make plain any need for a re-appraisal of policy. The DOE has made clear that it expects that any such alterations should be minor, made only as a response to fundamental changes in circumstances since approval. The DOE regional offices will regulate the

COUNTY	POPULATION (1981)	AREA (ha)	PERSONS PER HECTARE	POPULATION CHANGE 1971–81 %	STRUCTURE PLAN APPROVAL
AVON	909,408	134,614	6.8	0.4	
BEDFORDSHIRE	504,986	123,460	4.1	8.8	1980
BERKSHIRE	675,153	125,890	5.4	6.9	
– West					1979
– Central					1980
– East					1980
BUCKINGHAMSHIRE	565,992	188,284	3.0	18.8	1979
CAMBRIDGESHIRE	575,177	340,892	1.7	13.7	1980
CHESHIRE	926,293	232,846	4.0	6.9	1979
CLEVELAND	565,775	58,308	9.7	− 0.4	
– Teesside					1977
– West					1977
– East					1977
– Hartlepool					1980
CORNWALL & ISLES OF SCILLY	430,506	356,428		12.8	
– Cornwall					1981
– Isles of Scilly					
CUMBRIA	483,427	681,012	0.7	1.5	1980
DERBYSHIRE	906,929	263,094	3.4	2.3	1980
– Peak District					1978
DEVON	952,000	671,088	1.4	6.0	1981
DORSET (exc. S.E.)	591,990	265,375	2.2	6.8	1983
– South East					1980
DURHAM	604,728	243,592	2.5	0.4	1981
ESSEX	1,469,065	367,192	4.0	8.2	1982
GLOUCESTERSHIRE	499,351	264,266	1.9	6.9	1981
GREATER LONDON	6,696,008	157,946	42.4	− 10.1	1976
GREATER MANCHESTER	2,594,778	128,674	20.2	− 4.9	1981
HAMPSHIRE	1,456,367	377,698	3.9	6.1	
– South					1979
Mid					1980
North East					1980
South West					1982
HEREFORD & WORCESTER	630,218	392,650	1.6	12.5	
– Worcestershire					1975
– Herefordshire					1976
– Worcester City					1980
HERTFORDSHIRE	954,525	163,415	5.8	3.2	1979
HUMBERSIDE	847,666	351,212	2.4	1.1	1979
ISLE OF WIGHT	118,192	38,067	3.1	7.9	1979
KENT	1,463,055	373,060	3.9	4.5	1980
LANCASHIRE	1,372,118	306,346	4.5	2.0	
– North East					1979
– Central/North					1983
LEICESTERSHIRE	842,577	255,293	3.3	5.4	
– Rutland					1979
– Rest					1976
LINCOLNSHIRE	547,560	591,485	0.9	8.8	1981
MERSEYSIDE	1,513,070	65,202	23.2	− 8.7	1980
NORFOLK	693,490	536,776	1.3	10.8	1979
NORTHAMPTONSHIRE	527,532	236,737	2.2	12.6	1980
NORTHUMBERLAND	299,095	503,165	1.9	7.3	1980
NOTTINGHAMSHIRE	482,631	216,365	8.2	0.8	1980
OXFORDSHIRE	515,079	260,782	2.0	3.4	1979
SHROPSHIRE	375,610	349,014	1.1	11.4	1980
SOMERSET	424,988	345,094	1.2	10.0	1982
STAFFORDSHIRE	1,012,320	271,615	3.7	5.0	1978
SUFFOLK	596,354	379,663	1.6	10.8	1979
SURREY	999,393	167,924	6.0	− 0.3	1980
SUSSEX EAST	652,568	179,513	3.6	0.8	1978
SUSSEX WEST	658,562	198,935	3.3	10.9	1980
TYNE AND WEAR	1,143,245	54,006	21.2	− 5.6	1981
WARWICKSHIRE	473,620	198,054	2.4	4.0	1975
WEST MIDLANDS	2,644,634	89,943	29.4	− 5.3	
– Soluhull CB					1975
– Coventry CB					1975
– West Bromwich					1978
– Wolverhampton					1978
– Birmingham					1978
– Walsall					1978
– Dudley					1978
– Warley					1978
WILTSHIRE	518,167	348,070	1.5	6.5	
– South					1980
– North East					1981
– West					1981
YORKSHIRE North	666,610	830,865	0.8	6.3	1980
YORKSHIRE South	1,301,813	156,049	8.3	− 1.6	1979
YORKSHIRE West	2,031,510	203,912	10.0	− 1.5	1980

Development plan deemed to be a structure plan on approval.

Source: unpublished DOE statistics   OPCS. 1981 Census Preliminary Report for Towns

Table 3   County Characteristics and Structure Plan Progress in England

extent of these changes and supervise any necessary work.

Structure plan review is technically a separate activity but in most cases will emerge from the results of monitoring exercises. Many counties are now getting to the stage of comprehensive review, and in most cases this will lead to no more than a roll forward and fine tuning of existing policies. Counties which have experienced major economic downturns, like the West Midlands, are the most likely to oppose a roll forward, and will wish to submit major alterations. On the other hand, a few counties, such as Hampshire, have problems of accommodating new development that have prompted proposals to amend the existing plan. Only a very small number of authorities, such as Humberside, have considered completely new structure plans to replace those outpaced by economic change.

Progress and Conclusions

As indicated in Table 3, progress with structure plan preparation in England and Wales has been slow, because of factors such as the innovatory nature of the system introduced in 1968, the uncertainty over the scope and content of the plans, and the lengthy process of public participation. The delay between the 1968 Act and the completion of the process of local government re-organisation in 1974, accompanied by the consequent internal re-structuring also contributed to the process becoming rather drawn out. Even after submission, it has often taken two or three years for structure plans to acquire final approval. In Scotland, the implementation of the 1969 Act was delayed until after the re-organisation of local government in 1975, but progress has, nevertheless, been more rapid than in England and Wales. This can be explained by the greater precision and brevity of the Scottish plans, where many of the broader issues are identified in the *Regional Report*, leaving the Structure Plan free to concentrate on key issues for change.

Two types of structure plan can now be identified in Britain. Some take the familiar development plan form, consisting of policies to restrain and direct economic development in accordance with specific land allocation and environmental considerations. These are found primarily in southern regions and in those rural areas where it is possible to identify shared objectives, and where there is sufficient development to require guid-

ance and influence. In the economically depressed and deprived areas of the country, this form of planning is less relevant as there is little or no development. In such areas, major alterations to structure plans are now being proposed, rather than the slight modifications to policy that were initially envisaged as being all that would be necessary, and that the DOE expects.

Nevertheless, structure plans do provide a valuable point of reference for a variety of purposes, even though, looking back, we can see that structure planning has suffered an uneasy and at times embarrassed adolescence. The plans have been criticised for being too long, too detailed, too expensive and too conventional. Their policies have been seen, variously, as ambiguous, vague, unsubstantiated and platitudinous. We should, nevertheless, seek to place all these various criticisms in proper perspective. Structure plans, were, after all, conceived by the Planning Advisory Group in their wide ranging review in 1965 as part of an effort to improve the 1947 development plan system. As such they preceded the main debates on corporate planning (for which purposes they have been used), on public participation, and on the methodological and theoretical shifts that were to come about in the succeeding ten years. They also pre-dated local government re-organisation which bifurcated a planning system intended to be unitary. At the time of their inception there had been strong economic and population growth, rapid development and a sustained period of rising expectations. The intellectual, institutional, economic and social climate has changed radically since that time. Consequently, it would be possible to argue for yet further reformation of the system, even though structure planning is having to be re-defined as it operates – which is perhaps what we should expect anyway. This is not the place for a detailed discussion on the need for a new re-organisation of local government. However the proposed abolition of the metropolitan counties could be logically followed by the abolition of the shire counties. This and the need for co-ordination could argue their substitution by fewer regional authorities, better able to engage in the broader strategic planning implied by the structure plan process. Equally a closer and more responsive interface is needed between central and local policy-making, so that national policy is made more explicit, yet allows for a greater variety in local policies than has previously appeared to be the case from the degree of conformity required of many of the existing county structure plans.

2.3   LOCAL PLANNING

Local Plans

Local plans are normally produced by *district councils*, in accordance with the *development plan scheme* for a county, which details the coverage regarded as necessary. Local plans are required for those areas where structure plan policies need to be developed in more detail and related to specific sites. They are not needed for areas where little change is taking place and where the structure plan provides an adequate planning framework. Local plans may, therefore, be prepared at different times for different parts of a county as the need arises. In Scotland, however, local plans are mandatory and a full coverage is required by law (it is estimated that a total of 310 separate plans will be required).

Unlike a structure plan, a formal survey is not obligatory, but a similar procedure allowing public participation and consultation must be followed. The protracted and involved nature of the process (Table 4) has led to criticisms of unresponsiveness and to calls for reform. At times, progress seems to have been bogged down by a pre-occupation with the technical completion of each stage, while the general direction and purpose of the plan has been lost. Another difference is that objections are heard by a *local public inquiry* and not by an examination in public. The inquiry inspector submits a report on proceedings to the local authority whose planning committee consider any modifications they feel are necessary before formally adopting the plan. A local plan does not require the approval of the Secretary of State, but he must be informed of the steps taken to secure public participation, and has the right to call in the plan for detailed scrutiny. In preparing a local plan, the district council must have regard for the implementation of structure plan strategy, but under the 1980 Act they could be adopted in advance of structure plan approval. In these cases the county planners have a duty to consider whether adopted local plans actually do conform with their structure plans. Where there is a conflict between approved structure and local plans, the local plan prevails as long as there is general conformity. The local plan inquiry usually provides the means of settling differences on matters of interpretation.

The structure plan, together with its assembly of local plans, constitute the *development plan* for an area. This is legally binding, although there is a limited right of appeal to the High Court on matters of law and procedure. Despite its legal status, however, the develop-

Table 4   Stages and Timing in the Preparation of a Typical Local Plan

STAGES IN TYPICAL PLAN PREPARATION	TIMING IN MONTHS	RUNNING TOTAL
1. Preparation and publicising of local plan brief	1.5	1.5
2. Preparation of Report of Survey and associated public participation	18.0	19.5
3. Preparation of draft local plan and associated public participation	12.0	31.5
4. Production of 'final' version of local plan	2.0	33.5
5. Certification	1.0	34.5
6. Deposit	1.5	36.0
7. PLI	7.0	43.0
8. Inspector's report received	2.5	45.5
9. Modifications on deposit	4.0	49.5
10. Adoption of local plan	2.5	52.0
TOTAL	**52.0**	**52.0**

Source: M J Bruton et. al. Local Plan PLIs in Practice I. The Planner Jan/Feb 1982. Vol. 68. No. 1 p.16–19.

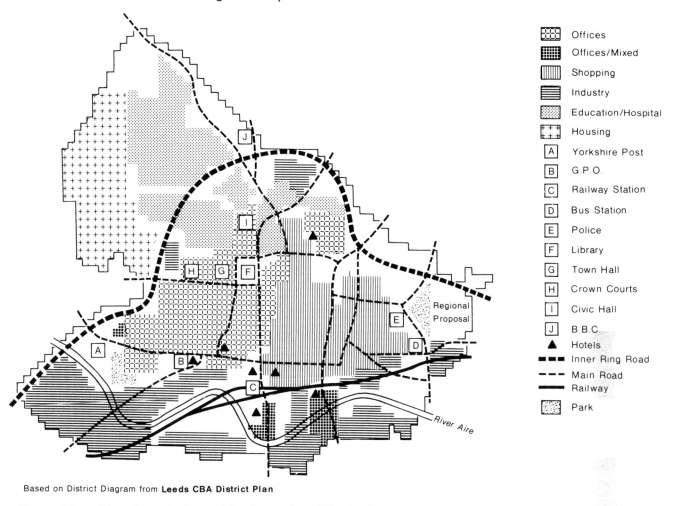

Based on District Diagram from **Leeds CBA District Plan**

Figure 2.5a   City of Leeds Central Business Area District Plan

ment plan does not automatically confer the right of development, i.e. although an area may be zoned for industry and a developer wishes to build industrial units, there may be good reasons why permission might still be refused. In other words, the planning authority need not always adhere strictly to the letter, but must have regard to the provisions of the development plan and can take other considerations into account. The development plan is thus a means of informing planning decisions, rather than determining them.

Although local plans can vary enormously in style and approach, there are three main types of plan:

District plans which refer to fairly large areas such as part of a sizeable town, all of a small town, or a rural area. The range of subjects covered in a district plan and an example of the scale of coverage can be seen from the diagram taken from the City of Leeds Central Business District shown in Figure 2.5a which shows in

diagrammatic form the major characteristics of the area. The precise form of district plan adopted will obviously depend on local circumstances, but essentially the choice lies between comprehensive district wide coverage and detailed sub-district treatment. The subjects that receive treatment are essentially the same as those contained in a structure plan, but the proposals are site-specific and effectively deal with local land management.

Action Area plans provide for the comprehensive treatment of areas identified as urgently requiring improvement, development or re-development within a ten year period. As the Sunnydale Action Area Plan in Derby shows (see Figure 2.5b on an adjacent page) these are even more specific both in terms of subject and of site.

Subject plans permit detailed investigation of a particular topic that cannot be adequately covered in a district plan or by the structure plan. Figure 2.5c gives some

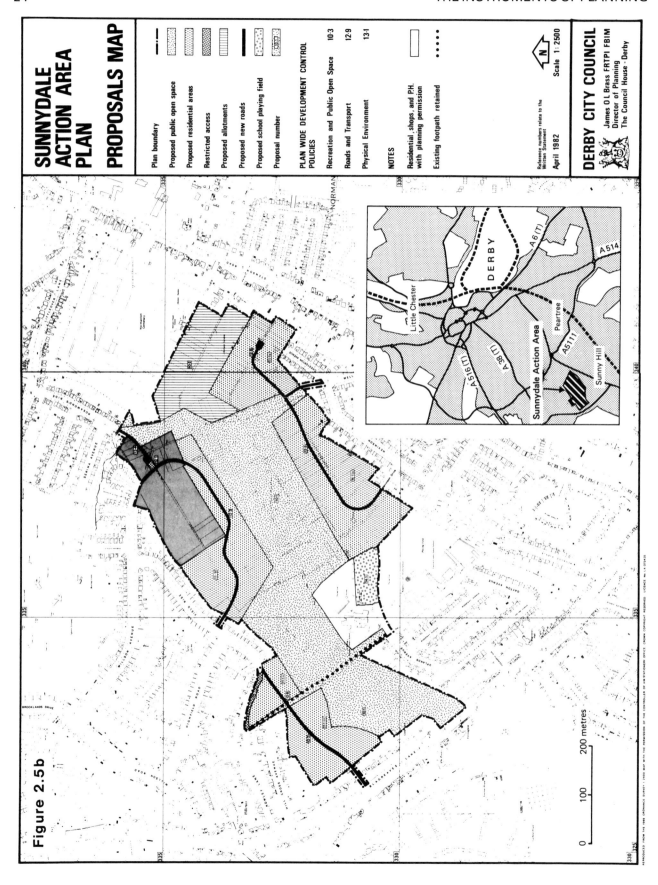

Figure 2.5b

SUBJECT PLANS HAVE BEEN PREPARED UNDER THE FOLLOWING TITLES:

Waste disposal	Green belt
Green belt and urban fringe	Recreation
Quarries	Mineral extraction
Coastal caravans and camping	Countryside and recreation
Minerals	Coast protection
Countryside	Brickworks
Agriculture and conservation	Recreation and conservation
Conservation and sand and gravel	Reclamation
Intensive livestock units	

Site specific subject plans have also been produced for areas such as river valleys, recreational areas, escarpments, coastlines etc.

Figure 2.5c   Subject Plan Topics

idea of the range of subjects dealt with in this way so far. It can be seen that only a small number of topics have been seen as suitable for treatment in this isolated manner.

Implementation

The local planning authority works towards its vision of the future by both positive and negative means. Little can be achieved in a *positive* manner without land ownership, and there are various mechanisms enabling local authorities to acquire land and develop it as they see fit, as well as to arrange for its disposal. These powers were briefly strengthened by the *Community Land Act 1975*, which would have required all land to pass through public ownership before it was developed. Any increase in land value realised by its development would then have been returned to the community. These powers were never fully implemented and the Act was repealed in 1980, although the Land Authority for Wales was retained and given its own powers of land acquisition. A *Development Land Tax* is still payable to the Treasury, but the principle of returning this gain to the local community no longer applies. Rather more specific powers are available to enable local authorities to achieve positive results in housing, transport, New Towns, National Parks, in Enterprise Zones, within Urban Development Corporations and for purposes of

conservation. These will be dealt with in more detail in Part Two. The positive side of development planning is often overshadowed by its restrictive and, at times, unpopular counterpart, *development control*. This is based on the principle of the 1947 Town and Country Planning Act which effectively nationalised the right to develop land, requiring owners to apply for permission to the local planning authority before developing their land. In the sense that development might be refused, the system appears to operate negatively but in fact development control is a key part of purposive planning, even if it is reactive rather than proactive in character.

The Development Control System

i) **Development**   The whole system of development control is totally dependent upon the legal definition of what constitutes 'development'. Under the 1971 Act, development is defined as *the carrying out of building, engineering, mining or other operations in, on, over or under land, or the making of any material change in the use of any building or other land.* The law goes further by specifying both extensions of, and exclusions from the definition. In particular, inclusion within the *General Development Order* (GDO), or the grant of a *Special Development Order* (SDO) has the effect of exempting certain types of development from the

Table 5 Permitted Development under the Town and Country Planning General Development Order 1977 (amended in 1980 and 1981)

Class

I Development within the curtilage of a dwelling house:

1. enlargement, improvement, alteration of dwelling house subject to certain volume, height and projection constraints.

2. construction of porch outside any external door subject to certain area, height and projection constraints.

3. erection etc. of any building or enclosure (except dwelling, stable, loose box or coach house) required for purpose incidental to enjoyment of dwelling house by its occupants, subject to certain projection, height, spacing and area constraints.

4. construction of hardstanding for vehicles incidental to etc. . . . . . .(as in 3)

5. erection of oil storage tank for domestic heating purposes subject to certain capacity, height and projection constraints.

II Sundry minor operations:

1. gates, fences, walls, subject to height restrictions.

2. means of access to highway.

3. exterior painting except for purposes of advertisement, announcement or direction.

III Changes of use:

1. to use as light industrial building (as defined by Use Classes Order)*from use as general industrial building.
*For details of the Use Classes Order see Table 6

2. to use as light industrial building (as defined by UCO) from use for purpose in class X of UCO.

3. to use for any purpose in class X of UCO from use as light or general industrial building.
2 and 3 subject to floorspace constraints.

4. to use as a shop for any purpose included in class I of UCO from use as shop for sale of hot food, pet animals and birds, motor vehicles, cats' meat shop, tripe shop.

IV Temporary Buildings and Uses

1. concerned with operations (except mining) for which permission already granted and applies to buildings, works, plant, machinery. Land must be reinstated afterwards.

2. use of land for any purpose on not more than 28 days in any calendar year (of which not more than 14 are used for motor car/cycle racing or for holding markets).

VI Agricultural buildings, works and uses.

1. building/engineering operations required for purposes of agriculture subject to ground area, height, projection and distance constraints. Does not include provision and alteration of dwellings.

2. roadside stands for milk churns.

3. winning and working on agricultural land of minerals required for agriculture including fertiliser and related works and buildings.

VII Forestry building and works.
Broadly similar to VI.

VIII Development for industrial purposes:

sidings, conveyors, sewers, mains, pipes, cables, plant, machinery etc. for industrial purposes (subject to certain scale requirements) so long as initial planning permission in force and external appearance of premises not materially affected.

IX Repairs to unadopted streets and private ways.

X Repairs to services.

XI War damaged buildings, works, plant.

XII Development under local/private Act of Parliament or Orders.

XIII Development by local authorities

1. to exercise duties as statutory undertakers

2. lamp standards, shelters, 'phone boxes, crush barriers, kiosks, etc.

3. deposit of waste materials or refuse on land used for that purpose on 1st July 1948.

XIV Development by local highway authorities or GLC. Maintenance and improvement works on existing highways.

XV Development by drainage authorities.

XVI Development by water authorities.

XVII Development for sewage and sewage disposal.

XVIII Development by statutory undertakers

1. railway undertakings,

2. dock, pier, harbour, water transport, canal etc.

3. water /hydraulic power:

4. gas

5. electricity

6. tramway/road transport

7. lighthouse

8. British Airports Authority

9. Post Offices

XIX Development by mineral undertakers

XX Development by NCB

XXI Use of aerodrome buildings

XXII Use as a caravan site

XXIII Development as licensed caravan site, XXII and XXIII subject to control under Caravan Sites and Control of Development Act 1960(a).

NOTE: This table contains only a crude summary of the GDO and for precise details the actual statutory instrument must be consulted.

(a slightly different GDO applies for Scotland under separate legislation)

Table 6:   Summary of the Use Classes Order 1972

Class I — Use as a shop for any purpose except as:-

a shop for the sale of hot food, pet animals or birds, motor vehicles, a tripe shop, a cats-meat shop.

Class II — Use as an office for any purpose.

Class III — Use as a light industrial building for any purpose.

Class IV — Use as a general industrial building for any purpose.

Class V. *Special Industrial Group A* — Use for any work which is registrable under the Alkali legislation of 1906, 1966 and 1971 and which is not included in any of Classes VI, VII, VIII or IX of this Schedule.

Class VI *Special Industrial Group B* — Use for any of a large number of metallurgical processes except a process ancillary to quarrying and mining activities.

Class VII *Special Industrial Group C* — Use for any of a large number of combustible processes except a process ancillary to quarrying and mining activities.

Class VIII *Special Industrial Group D* — Use for processes involving distilling, blending of oils; production or use of cellulose and other pressure sprayed metal finished with some minor exceptions; boiling of linseed oil and the running of gum; the use of hot pitch or bitumen; enamelling; production of certain chemical compounds and extrusion products, etc.

Class IX *Special Industrial Group E* — Use for carrying on any of a range of noxious industries, businesses or trades, e.g. blood boiler, bone grinder, candle maker, catgut manufacturer, dealer in rags or bones, fat melter, fish curer, glue maker, tallow melter or refiner, etc.

Class X — Use as a wholesale warehouse or repository for any purpose.

Class XI — Use as a boarding or guest house, or an hotel providing sleeping accommodation.

Class XII — Use as a residential or boarding school or a residential college.

Class XIII — Use as a building for public worship or religious instruction or for the social or recreational activities of the religious body using the building.

Class XIV — Use as a home or institution providing for the boarding, care and maintenance of children, old people or persons under disability, a convalescent home, a nursing home, a sanatorium or a hospital.

Class XV — Use (other than residentially) as a health centre, a school treatment centre, a clinic, a creche, a day nursery or a dispensary, or use as a consulting room or surgery unattached to the residence of the consultant or practitioner.

Class XVI — Use as an art gallery (other than for business purposes), a museum, a public library or reading room, a public hall, or an exhibition hall.

Class XVII — Use as a theatre, cinema, music hall or concert hall.

Class XVIII — Use as a dance hall, skating rink, swimming bath, Turkish or other vapour or foam bath, or as a gymnasium or sports hall.

NOTE: For precise details see the Statutory Instrument.

requirement of planning permission, which is deemed to be granted.

The GDO consists of standing orders applicable to all land nationally, and as can be seen from Table 5, it reduces the potential workload of local planning authorities quite considerably by exempting certain agricultural and forestry developments, certain domestic and other minor or temporary operations. In fact it was further amended in 1980 and 1981 for this purpose. Class III of the GDO refers to the *Use Classes Order* (1972), and this specifies 18 classes of similar use types within which change is permissible, but across which development may be involved if the change is *material*. It is considered material if a change of use 'matters' from the point of view of good and proper planning (Table 6). In practice this is an area of some difficulty (see Chapter 8) but legal precedents have enabled principles to be established which can be applied in cases of doubt.

An SDO applies only to a specified type of development or area of land such as that under the jurisdiction of a New Town or Urban Development Corporation. In addition, the 1971 Act, together with subsequent legislation, also imposes a number of *special statutory controls* over specific forms of development covering, for example, non-conforming uses, conservation areas, buildings of special architectural or historic interest, trees, the countryside, advertisements, minerals, caravans and waste land.

Building regulations are a different set of rules which relate to minimum standards of construction and do not relate to the controls imposed by town and country planning regulations. Applications are scrutinized for conformity to 1976 Building Regulations by a separate department and this process usually runs in parallel with that of seeking planning consent.

ii) Planning applications   Applications for planning permission must be made on an official form, accompanied by the appropriate plans and certain legal documents, together with the fee payable to the local authority (see Fig 2.6 on the pages that follow). Planning officers will advise on whether planning permission is required for a particular activity, but such advice is not usually legally binding on the authority. If planning permission is required then an *outline application* is often submitted in the first instance. In response, the local authority may give approval subject to being satisfied ultimately with the full details. A full fee is still paid for outline approval, but it does provide developers

with a reasonable assurance of obtaining full permission before they embark on the expense of having full plans drawn up. Before development may proceed, however, full approval must be acquired (within three years of outline approval being given) which will then be effective for a period of five years.

Applications must be dealt with by the 'appropriate authority', a decision made and the applicant notified normally within eight weeks of submission (Figure 2.7). The 'appropriate authority' is usually the district, but there is a requirement to consult with the county on applications of significance for structure plan policy e.g. minerals, waste disposal sites. Although the English counties lost their right to call-in applications under the 1980 Act, the Scottish regions have retained this power, but use it in only exceptional circumstances.

During this eight week period, the necessary consultations have to be carried out, the requisite advertisements placed, and the necessary site inspections made. Planning authorities are not statutorily obliged to notify people likely to be affected, but most do. All *material considerations* must be taken into account, including the development plan, before a decision is made. In cases where the development plan is incomplete, where no local plan exists and where there is no approved policy, accepted planning levels and standards of containment, conservation, density, comfort and nuisance are applied. In other words the planning authority must act in good faith. Although the local authority must be seen to be consistent in its decisions, each application must be considered on its merits as an individual case, and not prejudged in any way by any prior acts or statements – not even by the development plan itself.

iii) Appeals   In cases where planning permission has been granted but with conditions, or rejected outright, or if an individual feels aggrieved in any other way (specified by the 1971 Act), there is a right of appeal to the Secretary of State on *planning grounds* and also on matters of *law and procedure*. If the local planning authority and appellant are unable to come to some agreement on the basis of written representations, then a hearing or *public local inquiry* is held by an Inspector appointed by the Secretary of State. The Secretary of State is not obliged to accept the finding of the Inspector and any subsequent appeal may only be made to the High Court and on points of law and procedure.

iv) Enforcement   Although it is unlawful to develop without planning permission, it is not normally regarded as a criminal offence. A system therefore exists

Figure 2.6 Kirklees M.C. Application for planning consent (continued on page 30)

18439

KP 1

KIRKLEES METROPOLITAN COUNCIL
TOWN AND COUNTRY PLANNING ACT 1971
APPLICATION FOR PLANNING PERMISSION

Please read the notes for guidance before completing this form

Applications should be submitted by post to:

Directorate of Technical Services
(Planning Department)
Kirklees Metropolitan Council
P.O. Box B95
Civic Centre
Huddersfield HD1 2NA

Or handed in to the Head Office of the Directorate, Local Information
Office or Building Control Office

PLAN No.	
DATE OF RECEIPT	
RECEIPT No.	

PART A MUST BE FULLY COMPLETED Q1 - 20

1. I hereby apply for FULL PLANNING PERMISSION .... YES/NO
   OUTLINE PLANNING PERMISSION .... YES/NO
   APPROVAL OF RESERVED MATTERS (See also Q14) .... YES/NO
   RENEWAL OF EXISTING TEMPORARY PERMISSION .... YES/NO
   (i.e. A permission previously granted for a temporary period which has not yet expired
   (See also Q14)

I am aware that this application for planning permission will be dealt with entirely separately from any application which may be submitted for approval under Building Regulations (which is governed by entirely separate legislation and which may be granted despite the refusal of a related planning application or vice versa). Also that the local authority are in no way responsible for the consequences in the event of the work being carried out before any necessary planning permission has been obtained (or without regard to any conditions which may be attached to such planning permission) irrespective of any Building Regulation approval that may have been granted.

I enclose herewith a fee of £ .... in accordance with Part II Paragraph .... of the "Kirklees Metropolitan Council Schedule of Fees" under the Town and Country Planning (Fees for Applications and Deemed Applications) Regulations 1981.
OR
I claim exemption from fees in accordance with Part I Paragraph .... of the "Kirklees Metropolitan Council Schedule of Fees" under the Town and Country Planning (Fees for Applications and Deemed Applications) Regulations 1981.

Signed	On behalf of	Date

2. APPLICANT
   (Name and Address)

   Tel. No:

3. AGENT
   (Name and Address)

   Tel. No:

4. DESCRIPTION
   OF PROPOSED
   DEVELOPMENT

Area of site in sq. metres or hectares	Number of dwellings to be created (if appropriate)

5. LOCATION
   OF PROPOSED
   DEVELOPMENT

6. Is the application for an extension or alteration to an existing dwelling house where the occupant is a disabled person? .... YES/NO

   If YES complete the following Declaration:

   "I hereby declare that .... lives in the dwelling to which this application relates, and is a disabled person within any of the descriptions of persons to whom Section 29 of the National Assistance Act 1948(a) applies and that the proposed development is to improve his/her access, comfort, safety or health in the following way

   ....

   Signed .... on behalf of .... Date ....

PART A Continued

7. Is the application a revision of a previous application (made by the same applicant) that was:-
   (a) made no longer than 12 months ago and subsequently withdrawn? .... YES/NO
   or (b) refused no longer than 12 months ago? .... YES/NO
   or (c) dismissed on Appeal no longer than 12 months ago? .... YES/NO
   If YES, state previous application number

8. Has a previous application relating to the same site and proposed development been submitted within 28 days preceding the date of submission of this application? .... YES/NO
   If YES, state previous application number

9. Is this application submitted because "Permitted Development" rights have been removed by a condition attached to a previous planning permission? .... YES/NO
   If YES, state previous application number and condition

10. Is this application submitted for an approval under a condition attached to a previous planning application (other than reserved matters imposed on a previous outline permission)? .... YES/NO
    If YES, state previous application number and condition

11. Does this application seek the variation or removal of a condition imposed on a previous planning permission? .... YES/NO
    If YES, state previous application number and condition.

12. State: Means of Water Supply

Foul Water Drainage	
Surface Water Drainage	

13. State present use of land/buildings. If vacant last known use

14. If approval is sought for Reserved Matters or Renewal, state previous application number

15. If you are applying for OUTLINE PLANNING PERMISSION indicate the items for which you are seeking approval as part of this application

    SITING .... YES/NO
    DESIGN .... YES/NO
    EXTERNAL APPEARANCE .... YES/NO
    LANDSCAPING .... YES/NO
    MEANS OF ACCESS .... YES/NO

16. Is any felling, lopping or topping of trees involved? .... YES/NO

17. Does the development involve the construction of a new or the alteration of an existing access to or from a highway? .... YES/NO

18. The number of car parking spaces within the site.

19. The materials to be used externally

	EXISTING	PROPOSED
WALLS		
ROOFS		

20. Give details of any alterations or additions to original dwelling prior to this application (including detached garages)

PART B MUST BE COMPLETED IF THE APPLICATION INCLUDES ANY FLOORSPACE OTHER THAN RESIDENTIAL FLOORSPACE

State the following:

21. The nature of the industrial process/business to be carried on

22. Proposed total new floor space (by new building or change of use)
    (a) The amount of industrial floor space ....
    (b) The amount of office floor space ....
    (c) The amount of retail floor space ....
    (d) The amount of storage floor space ....
    (e) The amount of warehouse floor space ....
    (f) The amount of floor space common to both non-residential and residential uses (e.g. common service area)

    Sq. Metres

PART B Continued

23. The nature, volume and means of disposal of any trade effluents or trade waste

24. The number of employees:-
    Existing: MALES ————— FEMALES —————
    Additional: MALES ————— FEMALES —————

25. Is provision to be made for loading and unloading within the site?

26. Does the proposed use involve the use or storage of any of the HAZARDOUS materials mentioned in the Notes for Guidance? If YES state materials and approximate quantities (indicate storage location on the plan)

PART C YOU MUST SIGN AND DATE THIS PART AT QUESTION 29

27. **DECLARATION:** to be completed in all cases (delete either (a) or (b))

  (a) None of the land to which the application relates constitutes or forms part of an agricultural holding:

                         OR

  (b) I have/the applicant has* given the requisite notice‡ to every person other than myself/himself* who, 20 days before the date of the application, was a tenant of any agricultural holding, any part of which was comprised in the land to which the application relates, viz:-

    NAME OF TENANT   ADDRESS   DATE OF SERVICE OF NOTICE

  *Delete where inappropriate
  ‡A copy of the requisite notice is attached to the Notes for Guidance

28. **CERTIFICATES:** Complete relevant certificate in full. Inappropriate certificates should be deleted.

Please Note:
1. An owner is a person having a freehold interest in the land or a leasehold interest, the unexpired term of which is not less than 7 years.
2. Certificates C and D are only applicable if the applicant does not know the name and address of any owner and cannot therefore serve the requisite notice.
3. Copies of the notices referred to in Certificates B, C and D are attached to the Notes for Guidance.
4. You must sign and date your application at item 29 in addition to Item 1 in Part A.

CERTIFICATE A   I hereby certify that:-
No person other than the applicant was an owner† of any part of the land to which the application relates at the beginning of the period of 20 days before the date of the accompanying application.

                         OR

  *Delete where inappropriate
  † See note 1 above

CERTIFICATE B   I hereby certify that:-
I have/the applicant has* given the requisite notice† to all the persons other than myself/the applicant* who, 20 days before the date of the accompanying application were the owners† of any part of the land to which the application relates, viz:-

    NAME OF OWNER   ADDRESS   DATE OF SERVICE OF NOTICE

  *Delete where inappropriate
  † See note 1 above
  † See note 3 above

PART C Continued

                         OR

CERTIFICATE C
(b) insert description of steps taken
(c) insert name of local newspaper circulating in the locality in which the land is situated
(d) insert date of publication (which must not be earlier than 20 days before the application or appeal)

I hereby certify that:-

(i) I am/the applicant is* unable to issue a certificate in accordance with either paragraph (a) or paragraph (b) of section 27(1) of the Act in respect of the accompanying application dated:

  (a) ....

(ii) I have/the applicant has* given the requisite notice† to the following persons other than myself/the applicant* who, 20 days before the date of the application were owners† of any part of the land to which the application relates, viz:-

    NAME OF OWNER   ADDRESS   DATE OF SERVICE OF NOTICE

(iii) I have/the applicant has* taken the steps listed below, being steps reasonably open to me/him* to ascertain the names and addresses of the other owners† of the land or part thereof and have/has* been unable to do so:

  (b) ....
  ....

(iv) Notice of the application as set out below has been published in the

  (c) ....

  on (d) .... ENCLOSE COPY OF NOTICE AS PUBLISHED

  *Delete where inappropriate
  † See Note 1 above
  ‡ See Note 3 above

                         OR

CERTIFICATE D
Notes (b) (c) and (d) as for Certificate C

I hereby certify that:-

(i) I am/the applicant is* unable to issue a certificate in accordance with Section 27(1)(a) of the Act in respect of the accompanying application dated:

  (a) ....
  and have/has* taken the steps listed below, being steps reasonably open to me/him* to ascertain the names and addresses of all the persons, other than myself/himself* who, 20 days before the date of the application were owners† of any part of the land to which the application relates and have/has* been unable to do so:

  (b) ....

(ii) Notice of the application as set out below has been published in the

  (c) ....

  on (d) .... ENCLOSE COPY OF NOTICE AS PUBLISHED

  *Delete where inappropriate
  † See Note 1 above

29. **MUST BE COMPLETED**

SIGNATURE	ON BEHALF OF	DATE

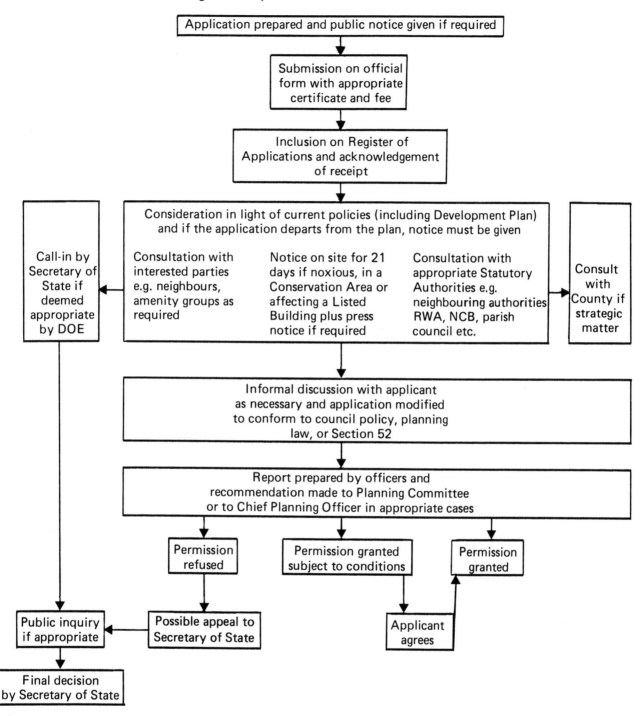

NOTE: In cases where a development involves erection, alteration, extension of
         a building, applications for planning permission must be accompanied by
         applications for consent under the Building Regulations 1976. In such
         cases a further fee is payable under the Regulations. Very little discretion
         is available to the local authority administering the Regulations.

Figure 2.7   An Outline of the Progress of a Planning Application

for the enforcement of planning law, and failure to comply is a criminal offence. An *enforcement notice* may be served where a local planning authority considers that planning control has been breached. In most instances, except those involving a material change of use, the notice must be issued within four years of the alleged infringement. An enforcement notice can be challenged by appeal on three grounds: permission should be granted for the offending development; a breach of planning controls has not occurred; the correct procedure has not been followed in issuing the notice.

If action required by an enforcement notice is not taken, then the offending developer is liable to prosecution by the local authority, or alternatively, the local authority can enter the premises and take any *default action* necessary to enforce their notice (except in cases where discontinuance of use is required). As a last resort the local authority can apply to the High Court for an *injunction* to prevent any continuation, and failure to comply constitutes contempt of court, and carries a threat of imprisonment. Since enforcement can be a protracted business, especially if an appeal is involved, the local authority can, with a few exceptions, issue a *stop notice* to prevent continuance of any of the activities prohibited by the enforcement notice. There is no appeal against a stop notice, and it is effective irrespective of any pending appeal against an enforcement notice. Failure to comply is punishable by a heavy fine.

This system of development control would seem to give the local planning authority an impressive amount of influence, but it must be remembered that their authority extends only to planning statute. Hence the phrase *material conditions to be taken into account* refers only to those aspects with land use planning implications. Although public distaste may have been expressed on the proliferation of 'sex shops', control can only be exercised on land use planning and not moral grounds. Equally, the range of conditions that can be attached to a grant of planning permission is restricted similarly. Apart from being reasonable in law, conditions must also relate specifically to the development in question, be capable of implementation, and not deprive owners of their existing user rights without compensation. Under *Section 52* of the 1971 Act, the planning authority may negotiate an agreement whereby a prospective developer might accept certain restrictions, or agree to provide certain facilities or amenities as part of the proposed development, in return for a grant of planning permission. In this way, concessions can be won that would not be legally acceptable if attached to a formal grant of planning permission as conditions.

Appraisal

i) **Local plans**   Encouraged by the promise of the local plan concept, extremely ambitious development plan schemes were drawn up. In 1975 they revealed an average of almost ten proposed local plans per authority. Since that time, a combination of factors have forced local authorities to revise their estimates so that two or three per authority is more likely. It can be seen from Table 7 that the number of local plans intended for England has not only been revised drastically but that there has been a swing away from action area and subject plans towards district plans, a swing which could be interpreted as a return to conventional land use planning and away from action-oriented intervention. Even at this reduced level, however, there still remains a con-

Table 7   Numbers of Local Plans proposed and produced for England 1974–82

Type of Plan	Local Plans proposed 1974-80	% of total	Local Plans proposed 1982	% of total	% reduced	Local Plans adopted or on deposit 1/3/82	% of total
District	1468	56	1149	83	22	172	80
Action Area	588	23	78	6	87	19	8
Subject	550	21	155	11	72	26	12
Total	2606	100	1382	100	47	217	100

Source: Based on statistics taken from M J Bruton 1983, Local plans, local planning and Development Plan Schemes in England 1974-82. **Town Planning Review** 54, 1, pp 4-24

siderable amount of plan preparation yet to be done, and pre-1968 development plans are still operative in many areas. Nevertheless, a great diversity of plans has been produced, the vast majority being district plans produced at a variety of scales for areas subject to some form of change or development pressure.

Unfortunately, local planning has not been the success story it promised to be in the 1960's. Plans have been criticised for taking an inordinate amount of time to prepare, for being inflexible once produced and for being costly. Much of the delay has been due to statutory procedure, the absence of approved structure plans, and the uncertainty surrounding the relationship between the two plan levels. Such doubts have been perpetuated by the process of structure plan review, which may result in the alteration or replacement of parts of the strategic framework for local plans. The survey seems to have been the slowest stage because of the need to acquire up-to-date information for the new districts, and to collect specialised data. The new district planning authorities must seek to inform themselves as to conditions in their areas, but some large scale data collection exercises have been undertaken without sufficiently defined ends in view. The 1980 Act requires local planning authorities to be selective in their preparation of local plans, but where a clear need exists, to proceed as rapidly as possible. To this end, authorities have been instructed to reduce their survey work, and to restrict public participation activity to the draft plan stage, at which point public interest is at its highest.

Partly in response to a changing political and economic climate, but also out of frustration with the statutory local plan process, a considerable amount of non-statutory planning activity is taking place, with some districts like those in Norfolk, for instance, doing more than others. This includes making *informal plans* for particular areas, *development briefs* for industrial regeneration, housing areas etc, and *policy statements* on particular topics. These have the advantage of being quicker and cheaper to produce that the statutory plans, as well as being more flexible and responsive in areas of rapid or complex change. But these plans lack legal foundation and hence do not perform well in appeal situations, lack credibility in the eyes of the public, and are not generally favoured by the DOE. The DOE advise that *supplementary planning guidance* of this kind be formally adopted by the local authority, and made subject to public consultation. In many cases, these non-statutory measures are used mainly as stop-gap devices, prior to the adoption of a statutory local plan. This is vital since it is estimated that at the current rate of progress, it will take 25 years to complete all the intended statutory local plans.

Local planning practice has had to respond to changing circumstances since the 1960's. Some authorities still face the problems of accommodating growth, but more have had to come to terms with the problems of stagnation or decline. Such changes have prompted a variety of practice, and have required an increased awareness and understanding of development processes, and the part that a local planning authority can play. In the changed situation, local planning has become more politicised, requiring an additional sensitivity on the part of officers. As with the Structure Plan at county level, so the Local Plan has been seen as a potential corporate planning tool, despite the fact that it is less generalised in its approach and more restrictive in its detailed application to matters of land use. Thus, while a large number of district authorities have attempted to operate in a corporate fashion, hoping to use the local plan mechanism, they have found themselves having to isolate land use planning matters for inclusion in the statutory local plan, and have failed to utilise to the full the information yielded by the local plan-making process.

ii) **Participation**   Local planning should offer the best possible opportunity for public participation. Public participation has mostly been canvassed at the survey stage, on completion of the draft plan, and by objection by the public at the local inquiry stage. This can take 3–5 years during which time the public cannot sustain a high degree of enthusiasm. The 1980 Act has, therefore, removed the need for participation at the survey stage, and for a public local inquiry if the local authority and the objectors can agree informally on modifications. Some have suggested that the public local inquiry should be dispensed with, as it has often proved a considerable delaying factor, but this would represent a fundamental change in planning philosophy. The right to a hearing operates throughout planning practice in the interests of natural justice and the rights of the individual. Even improved participation procedures would not necessarily obviate the need for an inquiry. The interests of individual parties can so easily be neglected or misrepresented, while fundamental differences of opinion will not be settled by any amount of participation. There seems to be general agreement on the need for public local inquiries in spite of their ponderous nature, with a strong feeling that the impartial recommendations of the Inspector should be binding on local authorities, who otherwise act as judge and jury in their own court.

iii) Development control This is the most contentious area of planning, since by definition it imposes restrictions on the freedom of owners to do as they wish with their own land and property. In some eyes the system imposes unwarranted restriction on matters of detail, while often offering only the vaguest of justification such as 'detrimental to amenity' (one of the most elusive yet fundamental concepts in planning!). By far the most common source of complaint, however, is the *delay* imposed on developers. It is argued that any delay is costly and that planning control can restrict the rate at which development takes place. In fact, though some local planning authorities do have a history of long delays, most reach a decision within the statutory eight weeks. Sometimes of course, delay is justified by the complexity of the application. A number of studies compare the performance of local authorities, and it seems, quite simply, that the fastest authorities are those with lower population densities and fewer applications. There is always a case for authorities to improve the efficiency of their working practices, as delays may add to a developer's costs. There is little ground for suggesting that this constrains the rate of development activity, since this is predominantly a function of local and national economic vitality. Encouraged by the apparent success of the Enterprise Zone concept there have been proposals to establish 'Simplified Planning Zones' in which only minimum controls would apply. This is despite evidence suggesting that any Enterprise Zone success has little to do with a simplified planning regime (see Chapter 4).

Analysis of statistics relating to the performance of local authorities can so easily distract attention from far more fundamental issues concerning development control. As with the planning system in general, development control is caught between two opposing ideologies. The first claims that development control should play an *enabling* role for private sector investment, imposing only minimal environmental safeguards. The second sees it as a much more *directive* activity, controlling and diverting private and public sector investment in socially and environmentally desirable directions. The 1980 Act relaxed the GDO in the spirit of the former role, identifying the planning system as an enabler of the private sector to re-build the economy, rather than as a means of placing unreasonable obstacles in the path of developers. However, it was felt that developers should pay an administrative fee for what is effectively seen as a development service.

Conclusion

Although it is still too early to evaluate the 1968/9 development plan system, for the success of local planning must lie in the extent to which its plans have been successfully implemented, a number of interesting trends are beginning to emerge.

There is an implicit assumption that development plan policies can, or will ultimately, be implemented through the development control system. The reality of the situation is often very different. Some policies are adhered to rigidly, but the limited powers of land use planning in Britain mean that many others have little chance of success. Some planning policies can be too flexible and 'open', so that many applications are determined with regard to 'other material considerations' and the development plan loses all meaning. The most successful development plans seem to be those produced in areas where development needs to be restrained rather than promoted. Planning powers are very effective in controlling the release and allocation of land for development purposes, but much less influential in performing all the other roles that local planning has acquired over the years. Development control has traditionally been *negative*, concerned with restriction in matters of amenity above all. In the absence of any meaningful *positive* powers, beyond allowing development, local authorities have found it extremely difficult to initiate and co-ordinate development, even in areas of growth, and thereby achieve full implementation of the development plan. In such a system a 'successful' plan will be that which most accurately anticipates the needs of developers, rather than any other party.

Much local planning, therefore, consists of responding to development initiatives from the private sector in the hope that this will eventually result in the implementation of planning policy. In effect, the local planning authority is far from central to, or in, the development process. The planning system's inability to produce results may be because of an increasing tendency to resort to informal planning methods and 'Section 52' agreements between planning authorities and developers; neither of these were intended to perform central roles. It may be that the existence of informal methods is a sign of positive response by the system. The use of Section 52 of the 1971 Act to exact what has been called *planning gain* has been condemned as cheque-book planning, planning behind closed doors, and even as blackmail. It has also been seen as a system of common-sense negotiation between developer and local authority to each other's mutual benefit. Such negotiation is by no means a novelty. Whatever the ethics, planning gain is one of the few ways in which local authorities can actively influence the development process in a positive way.

Planners have also been criticised for failing to understand how the development process operates, and for being unsympathetic to its needs and requirements. Certainly, the nature of the system is such that very few local authorities have become involved in the institution and direction of the full development process, from capital formation to the sale or letting of completed premises. Many authorities would find such a process politically unacceptable, believing that such procedures should be left in the hands of a developer, even though they may have an interest in the site. Instead, there is still a marked pre-occupation with standard local plan procedure as a rational and technical process with its own distinct stages. All too often, plan preparation is seen as something separate from development control, and the two aspects are managerially split in the working life of the planning department. This can too easily lead to neglect of plan implementation, although there are signs that lack of development pressure is forcing planners to look at the development process in much greater detail, and to identify roles that the local authority might perform effectively. The planning profession is beginning to recognise the need for greater imagination and innovation in local planning, but whether this can be achieved without a major overhaul of the basic machinery remains to be seen.

Lastly, while the development process includes the planners and developers as major actors, the stage is also populated by the general public. The statutory requirements for participation and consultation have met with only limited success because of the logistical difficulties in reaching the public at large, and because of the low level of concern for planning matters among the general public – or at least until their immediate interests are affected. It is at such times that 'action groups' are often formed, are sometimes successful, and occasionally continue in existence as local community watchdogs. The need for planners to have an awareness of public needs and preferences is shared by those in other public services; at least planning has seen some active expression of this obligation. The major difficulty, however, is that different groups in society have a very uneven access to decision makers. Organised groups such as local political parties, environmental groups from 'green' to Victorian, the CBI and TUC, and their local manifestations in Chambers of Commerce and Trades Councils are so structured as to make it relatively easy to respond to planning activities in an

authoritative fashion. At the other end of the scale, local action groups may attract attention, but not necessarily receive a serious response. Equally, the effectiveness of 'grassroots' community action whether on the part of residents' associations jealous of preserving local amenity or squatters anxious to secure a place in the housing market, is likely to have much to do with the political complexion of a local planning authority. This is a significant issue, since strictly speaking, it is the role of elected members to interpret the public will, for it is through them that the planners are responsible to the public. All the experience of the 1950's and 60's showed that this was an inadequate mechanism, but a satisfactory alternative has proved hard to identify.

Further reading

A simple introduction to the operation of local government is found in I H Seely 1977 *Local Government Explained* (Macmillan). For a convenient review see also P G Richards 1975 *The Reformed Local Government System* (George Allen & Unwin) and for a critique J Dearlove 1979 *The Reorganisation of British Local Government* (CUP) and A Alexander 1982 *Local Government in Britain since Reorganisation* (George Allen & Unwin).

A general introduction to structure planning can be gleaned from J B Cullingworth 1982 *Town and Country Planning in Britain 8th Ed* Chapter 3 (George Allen & Unwin), and from J Ratcliffe 1981 *An Introduction to Town and Country Planning 2nd Ed* Chs 3,4,5 & 6 (Hutchinson). More technical reviews of procedures and practice will be found in P Healey & M Elson 1982 The role of development plans in implementing planning policies *The Planner* Nov/Dec pp 173–177, I Bracken 1982 Problems and issues in structure plan review *The Planner* Jan/Feb pp12–16, and also Structure plans – submissions and alterations *The Planner* Jan/Feb 130–132, W Solesbury 1975 Ideas about structure plans, past, present and future *Town Planning Review* 46, 245–254, I Bracken & D Hume 1981 Forecasting techniques in structure plans *Town Planning Review* 52 and in D T Cross & M R Bristow 1983 *English Structure Planning* (Pion).

For local planning see Part 4 of J Ratcliffe 1981, as above, and for more detailed discussion *The Planner* 1982 Sept/Oct Special edition on Local Plans; the state of play, J F Garner 1981 *Practical Planning Law* chapter 7 onwards (Croom Helm), and Oxford Polytechnic 1982 *The Implementation of Development Plans* (Department of Town Planning Publication).

PART TWO
THE PRACTICE OF PLANNING

CHAPTER THREE
HOUSING

The modern system of town and country planning was largely born out of the efforts of a few pioneers at the end of the nineteenth century who aimed to create better living conditions, principally through better quality housing, arranged in a more spacious fashion on green field sites. Since this formative period providing good housing has been one of the major goals of town and country planning. Indeed, much of the early legislation joined housing with town planning in its title. It is salutary to realise, therefore, that the way this problem has been handled has proved to be one of spatial planning's most fundamental social impacts. The unwitting separation of public and private sector housing, massive suburbanisation and dispersal policies, along with the extensive use of high rise and 'industrial' building methods have played a major role in the creation of a significant set of social problems. These, with the continuing need to improve and replace the existing housing stock in the face of its natural deterioration, ensure that housing will always call upon planning skills – although land use planning alone is unlikely to provide solutions to the array of problems to which we have just referred. Nevertheless, the need to allocate land for housing (currently taking up almost 80% of our urban areas) remains. Housing is a commodity of vital importance, with the capacity to arouse deep emotion among politicians, planners and the public.

3.1   THE HOUSING STOCK

The number of dwellings has progressively exceeded the number of households in Britain since the early 1960's. As this has coincided with considerable improvement in housing quality since 1945, housing might no longer seem a significant problem, but in fact the definition of the 'housing problem' changes constantly as acceptable minimum standards are raised and the demand of the population for different types of houses shifts in relation to taste, financial means and household characteristics. Thus, while it is fair to say that Britain no longer has the same quantitative problem that it faced in the immediate post war years, concern is now focussed on an imbalance in the quality and distribution of different types of housing.

Quality   Figure 3.1 shows the apparent surplus of households over dwellings as well as illustrating the dramatic improvements there have been in housing quality since 1951, especially in the provision of basic amenities. On the surface, there would appear to be sufficient houses whose quality is improving all the time. The 1981 English House Condition Survey (1982) showed that this was not so. From a total of 18,000,000 dwellings, 1,100,000 were unfit and 900,000 were lacking in basic amenities. Allowing for overlap within these groups, approximately 10% of the total stock is nevertheless in need of improvement. Almost a quarter of the housing stock needs a minimum of £2,500 spent per house. Since many of these houses are pre-1919 stock, the average sum needed may be much greater. Problems are also now beginning to emerge in the inter-war and more recent stock, especially in public sector housing of the 1960's. The survey also revealed that for the first time there are more owner-occupied than private rented dwellings in poor condition, although the problems are greater in intensity in the latter group. These figures do not include Wales and Scotland, where the problem is certainly no better. In general, then, the problem is no longer the absence of basic amenities, although this feature still persists, but is the increasing amount of serious disrepair.

Distribution   It can be seen from Figure 3.2 that since 1961 the general picture has been one of growing owner-occupation, largely at the expense of the privately rented sector. There are regional variations, as shown, but the trend for most of Britain has been to restrict choice to either public rental or private ownership. A clear relationship exists between social class and housing tenure, with the semi- and unskilled groups accounting for the majority of council house tenancies. There is also a tendency for these groups to occupy those houses (public and private sector) lacking in basic amenities and needing repair most badly.

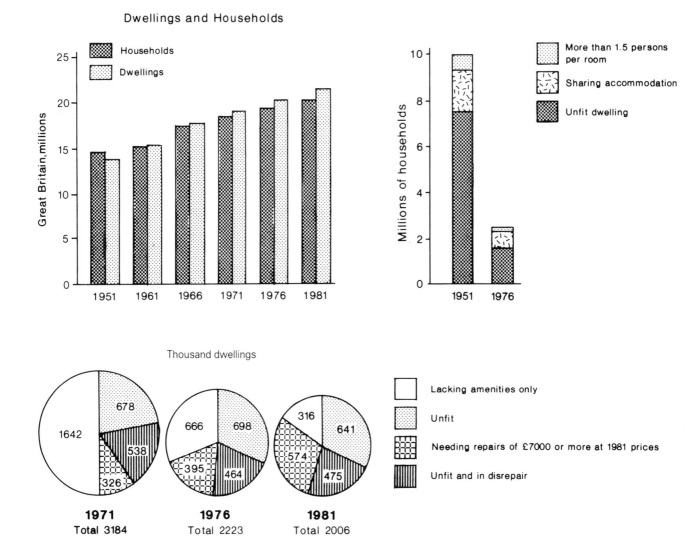

Source: HMSO **English House Condition Survey** 1981 Part 1, **Housing Survey Report** No.12. D.Bowers (1982) Aspects of the Housing Market, **Barclays Review** Vol LVII No.4, Nov.

Figure 3.1   British Housing Stock

3.2   THE HOUSING MARKET

Figure 3.3 portrays the kaleidoscope of factors which influence the geography of what is euphemistically referred to as the 'housing market'. It is difficult to quantify the degree of inter-relationship between the various factors, although they do divide neatly into factors of construction, exchange and occupation.

Demographic structure, rates of household formation, migration, stage in the family life cycle and the amount of disposable income are all important determinants of the demand for housing, but the range of choice available to meet that demand is constrained mainly by production and exchange factors over which planners or public exercise little control. In the matter of preference, for instance, owner occupation is seen as predominantly desirable, yet not all who wish to buy are able to do so. The majority of house-purchase loans are allocated by building societies, although banks, insurance companies and local authorities also offer mortgages. Loan applicants are selected on the basis of their stated ability to repay the loan within a specified period. Those people on low incomes, therefore, or on incomes which vary because of overtime, may be unable to become owner occupiers. Others may be effectively barred on grounds of age, or even sex, marital status

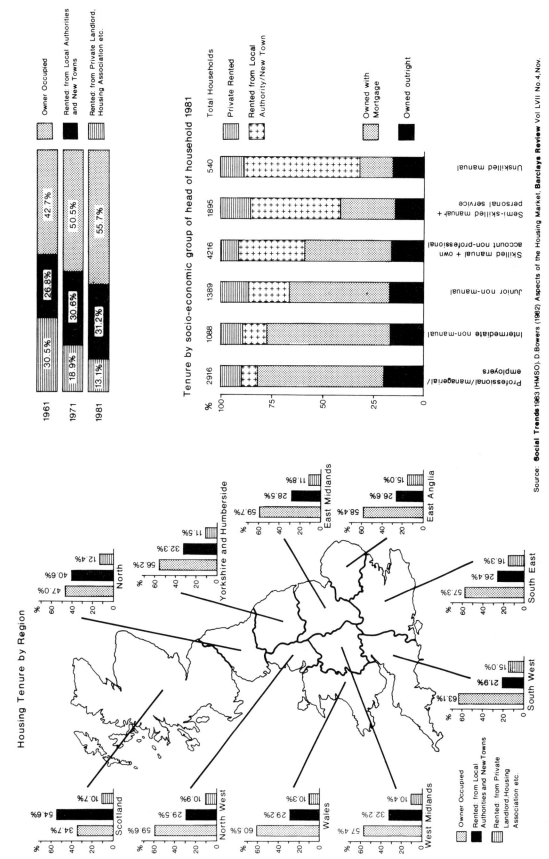

Figure 3.2 Housing Tenure in Britain

Housing Tenure by Region

Tenure by socio-economic group of head of household 1981

Source: **Social Trends** 1983 (HMSO), D.Bowers (1982) Aspects of the Housing Market, **Barclays Review** Vol LVII No.4,Nov.

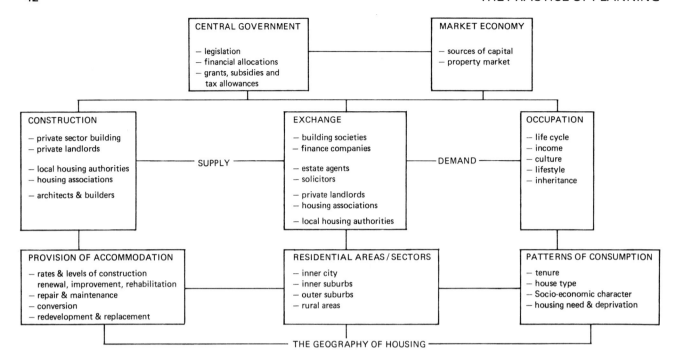

Figure 3.3   Simplified structure of the housing market

and race in so far as certain applicants may be afforded a lower priority by lending institutions. Building societies, in particular, were formerly less willing to lend on older, inner-city properties, but their activity in some inner-city areas is now much greater.

Those who are either unable, or unwilling to buy their own homes take up accommodation in the rented sector, predominantly from the district council which acts as the *local housing authority*. Households are entered with their requirements and preferences on a waiting list, and priorities are attached to different categories. This is a much more formal system of allocation than that which operates in the private sector, and for owner-occupiers, and is often criticised for its apparent arbitrariness. By choosing from its list the local housing authority is able to exercise some control over the social characteristics of particular housing estates. By such means the work of the local authority as planning authority and as housing authority interface. *Housing Associations* also operate a list system in offering units in various forms of tenure, and many of their tenants are nominated by the local authority, with whom they often have close links. Access to the *private rented sector* is determined almost exclusively by an ability to pay rent and is controlled by landlords or their agents.

In many cases, private renting is a short term measure for temporary residents, such as students, or for those who wish subsequently to buy their own house, or to rent from the local authority or a housing association. Because of all these factors, therefore, crude measures of the actual housing stock fall short of the housing stock effectively available to the public at any one time.

3.3   HOUSING AND GOVERNMENT

The state has played an increasingly influential role over the supply of housing since the Tudor Walters Report in 1918 advocated large scale building of houses for the working classes at certain minimum standards of density and amenity provision. The securing of adequate access to housing for the less well-off, and the maintenance of proper minimum standards for housing have been central policy issues ever since, and have deeply influenced not merely the supply of houses, but their visual appearance. Identical council houses on similar estates can now be found throughout Britain, proclaiming by their style the date of their construction. State intervention in the housing market goes much further, though, because the promotion of house owner-

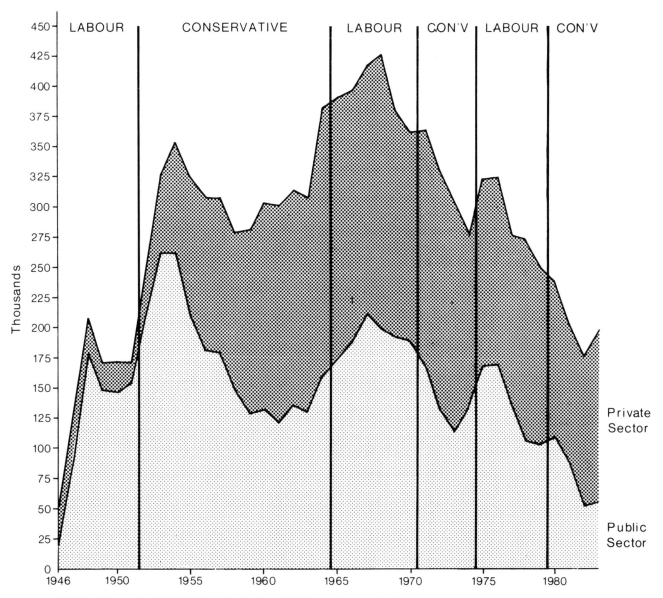

NOTE: Figures for 1946–51 for England and Wales only, rest for U.K.
Source: Data from D A McKay and A W Cox (1979), 'The Politics of Urban Change' and DOE 'Housing and
         Construction Statistics'

Figure 3.4   House building and political control

ship through fiscal methods has for long been an
assumption of government policy, while the house
building industry itself has often been used as a means
of government regulation of the economy.

Owner occupiers receive generous assistance in the
form of tax relief on mortgage interest payments, and it
has been shown that this 'indirect' subsidy is almost as
great as the more direct and obvious government expenditure on council house provision and rent relief. Since

the 1980 Housing Act, these benefits have been extended to council house tenants by giving them the right
to buy their homes as sitting tenants. Historical analysis
of housing provision in Britain reveals strong ideological preference for one or the other housing sectors.
With the exception of the early years of the 1951 Conservative government, the number of housing starts in
the public sector has tended to decline during periods of
Conservative office, while private house starts have
tended to hold up or improve.

In contrast, although the Labour governments have maintained their support for the principle of home-ownership, they have usually sought to increase the number of council house starts. This polarisation is reflected in the types and numbers of permanent houses completed during different administrations (Fig 3.4), and has led to the demise of the private rented sector, which now accounts for less than 13% of all tenure.

Government responsibility for housing lies in the DOE under a Minister for Housing and Construction, accountable to the Secretary of State for the Environment. The Welsh Office and the Scottish Development Department have responsibility for their respective areas. Central government influence over housing is essentially advisory and supervisory, exercised by statute and financial control, but at the broadest level it has found it relatively easy to control levels of investment in the house building and construction industry by specific controls on public expenditure on housing, and by exerting an influence on the price and demand for housing through the operation of the money market (in so far as it is able to control interest rates). The more specific aspects of housing management in the public sector are controlled by local government, with district councils performing the majority of functions, although the upper tier authorities do retain reserve powers. The GLC is an exception in that it is also a housing authority in its own right, along with its boroughs. A part is also played by the New Town Development Corporations in housebuilding.

The district council has responsibility for the provision, maintenance, letting (and selling) of public sector housing, and the treatment of unfit housing by clearance, rehabilitation or improvement. This is done through a local authority *housing department* in accordance with local needs. Housing departments are encouraged to take a comprehensive view of the situation in their own area, and are required to submit a detailed *Housing Investment Programme*, detailing strategy over a four year rolling programme. HIPs are presented annually to central government for approval and are used as a basis for making capital allocations. Many of the housing department's functions are performed in close liaison with the planning department, and often by inter-departmental teams also including environmental health officers and finance officers.

Housing and Planning

The requirement of land for housing will normally be taken into account in the preparation of structure plans.

As such, the kind of general requirements and principles included in Table 8 will inform the activities of district planners in relation to site. The mix, allocation, containment and area specific policies laid down for Gloucestershire are typical of housing inputs into structure plans. In rural areas the general policy for housing may well involve the implementation of a *key settlement strategy*, where housing is concentrated in certain key centres in order to achieve economies in construction and in the supply and maintenance of physical and social services. At the district level, planners are responsible for ensuring that sufficient land is available for housing, at appropriate locations. This is by no means a once and for all activity since requirements change and existing land uses may change somewhat as, for instance, existing residential land is re-used at a different density, or utilised for another purpose entirely. The tools available to the local planning authority include:

> local plans
> area based improvement policies
> development control

i) Local plans The very close relationship between housing and employment, transport, education, shopping and community facilities means that housing will be likely to figure in district and in action area plans. Particular types of housing needs and unsatisfied demand are identified from detailed surveys, primarily from a land use perspective. Areas of housing stress are earmarked for some kind of treatment. These are based on statutory definitions of 'unfitness' and carried out according to prescribed procedures covering compulsory purchase, consultation and compensation as laid out in Table 9. In the worst cases it may be necessary to invoke clearance procedures. Figure 3.5 provides an illustration of local plan coverage of housing matters. Housing policies for the central area of Darlington are shown in their structure and local plan context. In particular there is provision for rehabilitation, redevelopment and containment in accordance with plan objectives. Land availability is an important consideration in formulating policies, and close attention must be paid not only to the suitability of the location, but to the physical characteristics of the site along with the availability of access and necessary mains services. It is not unknown, for instance, for whole areas to be blighted for additional housing development because of inadequate sewerage and sewage disposal facilities.

ii) Area-based improvement policies Since the mid-1960's there has been a movement away from slum

Table 8   Gloucestershire County Council   Housing policies in the Structure Plan

PRINCIPAL POLICY H2
Residential development will be located principally at the main centres of employment.

PRINCIPAL POLICY H3
In areas of rural decline residential development, normally limited to infilling, and small groups of dwellings, will be encouraged in villages where additional housing can contribute to alleviating the causes of that decline.

PRINCIPAL POLICY H4
In areas not covered by Policy H3 residential development, normally limited to infilling and small groups of dwellings, will usually be permitted in those villages which have a primary level of local community facilities and services.

PRINCIPAL POLICY H5
In other villages residential development will normally be restricted to infilling.

PRINCIPAL POLICY H6
Isolated dwellings in the open countryside will normally be restricted to those which are essential to the efficient operation of agriculture and forestry.

GENERAL POLICY H7
Land for residential development will be identified so as to ensure at all times at least a 5 year supply of available land for house building in accordance with Structure Plan policies.

GENERAL POLICY H8
Existing planning permissions will not normally be revoked but applications for the renewal of permissions will be treated as new applications and will be determined in accordance with Structure Plan policies.

GENERAL POLICY H12
Provision will be made for residential densities to make the best use of land consistent with environmental considerations.

GENERAL POLICY H13
The refurbishment of existing dwellings will be encouraged and emphasis given to the inclusion of residential uses in the conversion of existing buildings and their renewal.

GENERAL POLICY H14
Further permission for residential caravan sites will not normally be given within areas of outstanding natural beauty.

These policies are then applied in more detail to the various geographical policy areas as below:

<u>CHELTENHAM POLICY AREA</u>

AREA POLICY H21
Provision will be made in the Cheltenham policy area for up to 8,500 dwellings between 1976 and 1996.

AREA POLICY H22
Within the Cheltenham urban area, and particularly the central area, priority will be given to the development of under-used land and buildings to accommodate in the order of 3,250 new dwellings between 1979 and 1996.

AREA POLICY H23
The conversion of residential accommodation to other uses will not normally be permitted, except where there are overriding environmental considerations.

AREA POLICY H24
Provision will be made to the south-west of the Cheltenham urban area for in the order of 2,250 new dwellings between 1979 and 1996.

AREA POLICY H25
Provision will be made at Bishop's Cleeve for up to 1,000 new dwellings between 1986 and 1996.

AREA POLICY H26
Elsewhere in the policy area new residential development will be in accordance with principal policies H4 and H5.

Source: Gloucestershire County Council Structure Plan March 1982.

Table 9   Clearance Procedures

1.   CRITERIA

Dwellings may be declared unfit by virtue of their state of repair, stability, natural lighting, dampness, ventilation, water supply, drainage and sanitation, facilities for cooling and disposal of wastes.

Clearance Areas may be designated by a local authority if the dwellings in an area are declared unfit, or the arrangement of the dwellings or street is dangerous or injurious to health and that the most satisfactory way of dealing with the problem is the demolition of all the buildings in an area.

2.   PROCEDURES

Compulsory Purchase may be used by a local authority within a clearance area, or adjacent to it so as to render the area convenient in shape or dimensions for re-development. Before making a CPO the local authority must be satisfied under the criteria above, be able to provide alternative housing and have the necessary financial resources for rehousing, demolition and re-development.

All persons with an interest in the property must be notified and a public local inquiry or private hearing led by an Inspector if there are objections. The Secretary of State may confirm or otherwise the Inspector's report.

Compensation Provision is made according to the interests of those involved and the state of repair of the property:

Owner Occupiers:	**Fit houses** — full market value, legal and valuation fees, home loss payments (if occupied 5 years or more)
	Unfit houses — site value and disturbance allowance, plus supplement to full market value if the property has been continuously lived in for at least 2 years, legal and valuation fees, home loss payments (as above)
Tenants:	Well-maintained payment, disturbance payment, home loss payment as above
Landlords:	**Fit houses** — full market value, legal and valuation fees
	Unfit houses — site value, well maintained payment, legal and valuation fees.

clearance and new construction in favour of rehabilitation and small scale infill development. Improvement grants for the installation of certain amenities in individual properties have been available since 1949 (even earlier in the pre-war Development Areas), subject to certain conditions of eligibility as shown in Table 10. Of the four types of renovation grant shown, only the intermediate is available as of right, with the rest left to the discretion of the local authority.

Under the provisions of the 1969 Housing Act, the level of grants was increased, and the concept of the General Improvement Area (GIA) was introduced, within which financial support would be available not only for housing, but also for such environmental improvements as the provision of parking spaces, playgrounds and tree planting. The local authority thus has access to central funds for the provision of facilities which it would not otherwise provide, and which would not normally be provided by existing private owners. Area based improvement received an additional fillip in the 1974 Housing Act, which empowered local authorities to designate *Housing Action Areas* (HAA) for areas of severe housing stress and deprivation. These are areas not likely to be relieved by GIA designation, a measure usually reserved for areas of mixed housing quality, with greater potential for self-improvement. The 1974 Act, in particular, provided local authorities with wide-ranging powers and financial support to remove the cause of housing stress and to produce quick and effective 'housing action'. A five year time limit is imposed for an HAA improvement programme, and such a

PROPOSALS AND POLICIES

POLICY H1 THE RESIDENTIAL AREAS

The following residential areas will be protected against the undesirable effects of non-residential uses located within or near them. Changes from residential to non-residential uses will not normally be permitted:

East Raby Street area
Raby Street area
Outram Street area
Hargreave Terrace area

Sun Street
Lodge Street area
Borough Road (N) area

In addition to protecting the amenity of the residential areas, the Borough Council will take positive steps to improve existing environmental conditions by utilising GIA proceedings.

POLICY H2 BOROUGH ROAD (SOUTH) MIXED-USE AREA

Changes from residential to non-residential uses will not normally be permitted.

POLICY H3 GLADSTONE STREET AREA

Changes from residential to non-residential uses will not normally be permitted in the Gladstone Street area (west of North Lodge Terrace) except as provided for in Policy S3.

POLICY H4 EXTENSIONS TO TERRACED HOUSES

First floor extensions to terraced houses will only be permitted where there will be no serious adverse effect on the amenity of neighbouring dwellings.

PROPOSAL H5 SITES FOR NEW HOUSING

New housing development will take place at the following sites:

7–31 Outram Street (odd numbers)
32–46 Outram Street (even numbers)
1–55 Wycombe Street and 1–3 Outram Park (all odd)
Kendrew Street car park

POLICY H6 OTHER NEW HOUSING DEVELOPMENT

New housing development will normally be permitted in the central area provided that a satisfactory residential environment can be attained and another use is not more appropriate for the site. Developers will be encouraged to incorporate residential accommodation within commercial development schemes wherever possible.

POLICY H7 UPPER FLOORS IN COMMERCIAL PROPERTY

The change of use of upper floors in commercial property to residential accommodation will normally be permitted provided that a satisfactory residential environment can be attained.

POLICY H8 SUB-DIVISION OF LARGER DWELLINGS

The sub-division of larger dwellings will normally be permitted where there will be no adverse effect on the amenity of nearby dwellings.

Figure 3.5   Darlington DC Central area local plan (simplified extract)

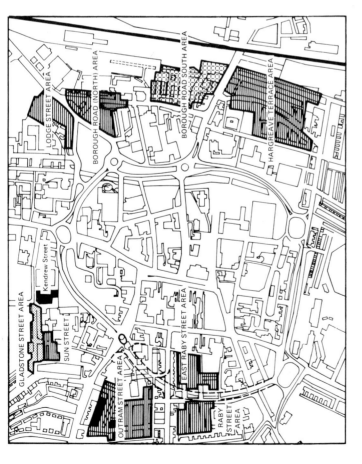

Policy/Proposal

(H1)

(H2)

(H3)

(H5)

▦ Residential area to be protected and improved

▨ Borough Road (south) mixed-use area

▧ Gladstone Street area

■ Sites for new housing

STRUCTURE PLAN CONTEXT

The Urban Structure Plan aims to keep the loss of population from the inner area of Darlington to a minimum. It proposes that this should be done by: rehabilitating areas of older housing; redeveloping suitable vacant sites for new housing; minimising the number of dwellings lost in redevelopment schemes; and, where appropriate, seeking the provision of residential accommodation in other forms of development.

LOCAL PLAN OBJECTIVES

– To minimise the loss of population from the central area

– To protect and improve the amenity of existing housing

– To identify opportunities for new housing

Table 10 Home improvement grants 1983

Renovation grants	Improvement	Intermediate	Special	Repair
1 Purpose of grant	Available at the discretion of LA for improvement or conversion of dwellings to modern standards or, in cases of hardship, partial improvement	Available as of right (subject to conditions below) for provision of some or all of the standard amenities, and for associated repairs if the applicant wishes.	Available at the discretion of LA for provisions of more standard amenities in HMOs, and for means of escape from fire, and associated repairs. But see (11) below.	Available at discretion of LA for substantial and structural repairs only. But see (11) below.
2 Maximum eligible expense	*Priority cases* £10,200 (£11,800 per dwelling for conversions of houses of three-storeys or more) in Greater London (GL) £13,800 (£16,000) *Non-priority cases* £6,600 (7,700 in GL £9000 (£10,400) The maximum percentage of the eligible expense allowed for repairs (where house is in need of substantial and structural repairs) is 70%; otherwise 50%	£5275 max.(2275 for specified sums for each of seven specified amenities and £3000 for repairs) in GL £7205 (£3005 and £4200). For reduced standards of repair £300 (£420 in GL) times number of amenities up to a maximum of £1200 (£1680 in GL)	As intermediate grants for specified amenities (but more than one of each may be allowed) and for repair. For means of escape from fire £8100 (£10800 in GL)	£4800 (£6600 in GL)
3 Maximum grant rate	*Priority cases:* 75%, but in cases of hardship up to 90%; *Non-priority cases:* 50%, but in cases of hardship up to 65%. For houses in GIA's 65%.			All are *priority cases*
4 Central government contribution	*Priority cases:* 90% of grant paid *Non-priority cases* 75% of grant paid			
5 Minimum life	Thirty years. LA discretion to reduce to ten years	Not specified, but for short life properties reduced repair standards encouraged	LA discretion	LA discretion
6 Standard	Ten-point standard with LA discretion to reduce; repair standard 'reasonable', with LA discretion to reduce	Reasonable repair and fit — can be reduced at LA discretion	LA discretion But see (11) below	Reasonable But see (11) below
7 Rent increase allowed to private landlord	Where landlords carry out work they can apply for new 'fair rent' with increases phased over two years. Where tenants fund improvement, landlords cannot increase rent on basis of tenants' expenditure.			
8 Occupancy conditions	(i) If grant paid to *private landlord* dwelling has to be let for five years, or otherwise grant to be repaid at LA discretion (ii) If grant paid to *tenant,* no repayment can be imposed on him but private landlord may have been required to meet letting conditions in (i) above. (iii) If grant paid to *owner*-occupier dwelling has to remain occupied by existing owner of close relative for five years or can be sold to another owner-occupier, or can be let after first year – otherwise repayment at LA discretion			
9 Land tenure	Owner of freehold, or five years unexpired lease, regulated (private) tenant, secure (public) tenant			
10 Age of house	Pre-1961 (except for works for disabled persons)		Not applicable	Pre-1919
11 Compulsory improvement/repair	Not applicable	Improvement notice at LA discretion where tenant requests and house lacks one or more amenities. Reduced standard can apply	Where notice under S.15 of Housing Act, 1961 or Sch.24 of Housing Act 1980 served, grant becomes mandatory	Where repair notice served under S.9 of Housing Act, 1957, grant becomes mandatory
12 Rateable value limits for owner-occupied houses	For improvements £225 (£400 in GL). For conversion £350 (£600 in GL) Not applicable in HAAs or for works for disabled persons	Not applicable		£225 (£400 in GL)

Priority cases	Ten-point standard	Standard amenities
(i) dwellings or HMOs in HAAs; (ii) dwellings or HMOs which are unfit for human habitation; (iii) dwellings which lack one or more standard amenities and HMOs which lack sufficient standard amenities for the occupants; (iv) dwellings in need of substantial and structural repairs; (v) HMOs which lack adequate means of escape from fire, where the works remedy the condition in question.	(i) be subsequently free from damp. (ii) have adequate natural lighting and ventilation in each habitable room (iii) have adequate and safe provision throughout for artificial lighting and have sufficient electrical socket outlets for the safe and proper functioning of domestic appliances; (iv) be provided with adequate drainage facilities; (v) be in stable structural condition; (vi) have satisfactory internal arrangement; (vii) have satisfactory facilities for preparing and cooking food; (viii) be provided with adequate facilities for heating; (ix) have proper provision for the storage of fuel (where necessary) and for the storage of refuse; (x) conform with the specification for the thermal insulation of roof spaces laid down in the Building Regulations in force at the time of grant approval.	(i) fixed bath or shower; (ii) hot and cold water supply at fixed bath or shower; (iii) wash-hand basin; (iv) hot and cold water supply at wash-hand basin; (v) sink; (vi) hot and cold water supply at sink; (vii) water closet.

(HMOs — Houses in multiple occupation)

Source: after M S Gibson & M J Langstaff (1982) An Introduction to Urban Renewal, Hutchinson

	LOCAL AUTHORITY	OTHER AUTHORITIES	RESIDENTS
DECLARATION	GIA Working Party established, including representatives of Housing, Environmental Health Architecture/Planning, Engineering, Chief Executive/Finance.	Informal consultation with DOE leading to full declaration.	House to house surveys and formation of Street Groups/Residents' Association.
PLANNING	As above plus detailed work in departments.	Loan sanction and grant approval from DOE. Consultation with County/Area authorities re Planning, Highways, Social Services, Education, Emergency Services. Consultation with statutory undertakers.	Meetings and promotional work with Street Groups/Residents' Association, including preparation of Show House and involvement of commercial firms. Public Inquiries on Compulsory Purchase Orders if required.
IMPLEMENTATION	On-site work by direct-labour/contractors supervised by appropriate officers.	Grant aid received from DOE. Highway works undertaken by County. Statutory undertakers lay sub-surface services.	House grants processed.

Table 11   Stages in GIA implementation

programme is likely to contain compulsory action on the part of private owners (who are of course grant-aided in their improvements). *Priority Neighbourhoods* may also be designated around GIAs and HAAs in an attempt to avoid the spread of deterioration. Such neighbourhoods are not eligible for grants for environmental work, however, and simply allow the local authority to exercise rights of land acquisition similar to those of HAAs as appropriate. The success of these area-based policies is dependent upon the level of financial support received by local authorities to enable them to make substantial grants to private owners. Government support stands at 90% in HAAs and 75% in GIAs. The formation of housing associations to work in such areas was also encouraged by the allocation of extra funds to the *Housing Corporation*, the fringe body set up in 1964 to channel funds and offer advice to the voluntary housing sector. In 1982 approval was given for local authorities to carry out *envelope schemes* to improve whole blocks of houses in HAAs. This involves exterior renovation of a complete block of houses to provide a secure 'envelope' sufficient for 30 years life, whether interiors are improved or not. It is hoped that this approach will avoid the patchiness that often results from the sporadic take-up of grants.

The role of the local planning authority in all of this is mainly in the identification of areas of physical deterioration, and in undertaking environmental schemes, probably as part of a GIA working party of the type identified in Table 11. The planning authorities (district and county) play an integral but quite limited role in the process of implementation. Housing stress, as such is mainly the province of a local *housing* authority, or a matter for Environmental Health, and it is they who are principally responsible for the administration and implementation of grant applications and internal improvement works. District planning authorities with inner city problem areas have also been involved in various projects, some emanating from the government's *Urban Programme*. This has involved carrying out need assessment programmes, and implementing improvement projects, often by mobilising private sector investment. Innovations in this area have included the subsidisation of private house construction for sale, and 'improvement for sale' schemes.

iii) Development control   The procedures outlined in Chapter 2 enable local planning authorities to exercise their powers of development control over private housebuilders and developers. Technically, development will only be permitted in accordance with the housing policies contained in the development plan, but disputes occur frequently. These usually relate to take-up of agricultural or greenbelt land, or arise over the amounts and location of land allocated for housing. The vagaries of forecasting housing demand means that the accuracy of the predictions made by the planning authority is often debated. (The local planning authority has to identify five year's supply of land for private house-building at all times.) Planners are usually keen to see their proposed levels accepted, not only for environmental reasons, but also because of the implications that an increase could have for the provision of shopping, transport, education and other ancillary facilities. On the other hand, private housebuilders have a vested interest in securing an allocation that enables them to build as many houses, in as many desirable locations as they think the market will bear.

The extent to which planning authorities influence the design and appearance of housing has been regulated by a series of DOE circulars. They can reject obviously poor designs which are out of character with their surroundings, but must confine themselves only to those aspects of design, layout and density significant for the aesthetic quality of areas as a whole. This is clearly a highly debateable matter of taste, heightened in sensitive locations, such as National Parks, by additional powers relating to details of design and construction. Many authorities, particularly in sensitive areas, have produced *design guides* for prospective developers in an attempt to improve the quality of the built environment. While these may be influential, they are not legally binding, and attempts to include them in full within development plans have usually been unsuccessful. However, some influence can be exerted over such matters by issuing planning briefs for specific sites outlining the form of development which would be favoured by the planning authority. Planners have been strongly criticised, especially by the Housebuilders' Federation, for attaching detailed conditions to grants of planning permission, but others see this degree of control as essential for the maintenance of high standards of visual amenity.

3.4 CONCLUSION

Housing policy in Britain is much more diffuse than in many European countries. This makes the function and impact of the various participants in the housing market much more difficult to define and evaluate. The local planning authority's role in the housing field can be summarised as ensuring that the claims on land use for housing purposes are reconciled with other planning considerations, and as supporting housing/environmental health departments in improvement and rehabilitation schemes. Nevertheless, the implementation of such housing policies, as part of development plans since 1947, has changed the face of Britain.

Slum clearance and dispersal, zoning and allocation, green belt restrictions and the accommodation of 'overspill population' in expanded and new towns have all left their mark. In particular, policies of *containment*

have given building land a scarcity value which affects the consumer in higher prices and higher site densities. Alternative policies would of course have accrued other costs. However, there are large areas of the housing market for which the planner is not responsible, not least its specific architectural form and tenure.

Since 1945, the emphasis has shifted, in turn, from the need to build new houses, through replacement and slum clearance, to limited replacement and rehabilitation by the late 1960's. During the 1970's, improvement policies expanded from concern with the physical structure of individual dwellings to packages aimed at improving the wider social framework of particular areas. This trend called for some form of interdepartmental corporate strategy but as this did not include the private housebuilder there have been moves in the 1980's to involve the private sector which it is hoped will result in a more integrated approach. Thus local authorities increasingly put together comprehensive improvement packages for large areas, sometimes derelict, involving commercial, light industrial and housing development. Various partnership agreements with the private sector have been set up for the renewal of council estates. Nevertheless, correlating projected demand and current rates of deterioration indicates that current efforts will be insufficient to avoid a shortfall of appropriate housing in the 1990's without more resources and greater central government commitment to housing generally.

Further reading

A useful introduction to housing and the housing market is found in L McDowell 1982 Urban Housing Markets, Unit 12 *Open University Course D202 (Urban Change and Conflict)*. For a more detailed and largely apolitical coverage see D Donnison and C Ungerson 1982 *Housing Policy* (Penguin). Detail of party-political influences on housing in Britain can be found in D H McKay & A W Cox 1979 *The Politics of Urban Change* Chapter 4 (Croom Helm). For further information on housing renewal and rehabilitation see M S Gibson & M J Langstaff 1982 *An Introduction to Urban Renewal* (Hutchinson). A disturbing view of renewal performance is put forward by M Gibson and J Perry 1984 Housing renewal in crisis, *The Planner* (April). Comprehensive treatment of the subjects can be found in S Merrett 1979 *State Housing in Britain* (Routledge & Kegan Paul), S Lansley 1979 *Housing and Public Policy* (Croom Helm) and J R Short 1982 *Housing in Britain: the post war experience* (Methuen).

CHAPTER 4
EMPLOYMENT

Satisfying remunerative work is a major goal for life for most of the population, yet it is one which has been denied to more and more people as unemployment levels have risen since the early 1970's, a phenomenon which as Figure 4.1 shows, had its origins much earlier. The changing pattern and structure of employment must affect land use and planners have sought to grapple with this issue, which is fundamental to any community's well-being. In many ways the unemployment problem illustrates *the* major dilemmas for modern planning: a system which is based upon development cannot respond adequately to circumstances of contraction; and a set of controls which are essentially spatial and local have little relevance to or impact upon a problem which is structural and of much wider consequence.

4.1 EMPLOYMENT CHANGE

The high technology of advanced capitalism, the oil crisis, the over-valuation of Sterling, the world recession and low levels of managerial efficiency have all been blamed for British employment change. Whatever the causes, the impact of recession has been devastating with no industry, region or sub-region being completely immune. In this respect the problem is much more widespread than it was in the inter-war years. Much of the decline in the *employed labour force* has been in the primary and manufacturing sectors, which has meant that the worst effects of recession have hit the inner urban areas and, especially, the industrial conurbations. Except in wartime, employment in primary industries, however, has been declining for most of the present century. As shown in Fig 4.1, the manufacturing sector experienced alternate growth and decline up to the early 1970's when the decline became continuous. By contrast, service employment has expanded consistently up to 1979–80 (providing many part time jobs for women), but since then has joined manufacturing in a decline.

Another major trend which has affected employment levels is the increase in the *working population*, mainly due to the greater number of women seeking employment, but as jobs have become more scarce, many female workers (especially married women) have become discouraged from seeking employment so that the number officially recorded as 'looking for work' has declined since 1979. What the official statistics demonstrate unequivocally is the demographic and regional unevenness of unemployment; the highest unemployment rates are found among the youngest and oldest age groups and among ethnic minorities. The distinctive industrial structures of the various regions of Britain has meant that they have been affected by the recession in different ways and to varying degrees, and it can be seen in Fig 4.2 that even the traditionally prosperous South East and East Anglia have been hit, albeit less than the older manufacturing regions. There have also been changes at an intra-regional scale. Historically most employment opportunities have been located in or near the cores of our urban areas, but since the 1960's these areas have increasingly lost jobs to the metropolitan rings and to small and medium sized towns in neighbouring semi-rural and more attractive locations. This is particularly apparent in the remaining belt of sustained growth stretching in a broad arc from Exeter to the Wash and pierced by an arrow of considerable development pressure running westwards from Heathrow along the line of the M4. At the finer grain, however, such broad patterns are less noticeable, and at local level much greater variation can be caused by seasonal changes, technological developments, and the changing fortunes of single major employers.

Across the whole industrial economy, however, lies a less obvious geography of industrial control. Put briefly, declining manufacturing firms are more subject to take-overs and mergers, with the effect that many formerly independent companies in the traditional manufacturing areas have become off-shoots or branch plants of larger, often international, organisations. This makes them subject to wider policy making relating to investment within the group as a whole, so that they may suffer further 'rationalisation' according to the

Figure 4.1 Employment levels

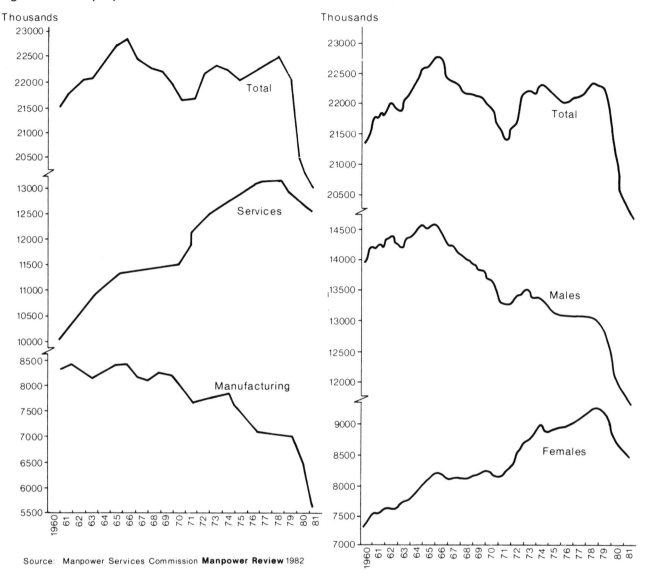

Source: Manpower Services Commission **Manpower Review** 1982

policies of the parent company. A secondary and related aspect is that U.K. head offices tend to be based in or near London. This has the effect of increasing the vulnerability of provincial branch units, while decreasing the numbers of financially skilled personnel in such areas. Since new businesses are more likely to be started by such people, the 'geography of innovation' may thus be skewed away from the most vulnerable regions in favour of the more prosperous.

4.2 PLANNING FOR EMPLOYMENT

Central Government

Central government has a long tradition of regional policy aimed at encouraging industry to move to less prosperous areas. These efforts have been criticised for being too expensive in terms of the numbers of jobs

LOCAL STATISTICS
(areas with more than 20% unemployment at April 1984)

SOUTH EAST

Sheerness	20.2

EAST ANGLIA

Hunstanton	30.3

SOUTH WEST

Falmouth	20.3
Ilfracombe	27.2
Newquay	24.5
Penzance	20.0
St. Ives	25.0

WEST MIDLANDS

Oakengates	20.3

EAST MIDLANDS

Mablethorpe	24.2
Skegness	22.1

YORKSHIRE & HUMBERSIDE

Mexborough	22.4
Whitby	21.7

NORTH WEST

Ormskirk	21.5
Widnes	20.7

NORTH

Consett	24.3
Hartlepool	22.6
Teeside	20.2
Wearside	21.0

WALES

Bargoed	20.0
Cardigan	20.8
Ebbw Vale	20.7
Holyhead	22.4
Lampeter	25.9
Pembroke Dock	26.1
Rhyl	21.0
Tenby	28.6
Tywyn	20.4

SCOTLAND

Anstruther	21.4
Arbroath	21.7
Dumbarton	20.8
Forres	22.5
Irvine	22.8
North Lanarkshire	20.5
Portree	20.9
Rothesay	21.1
Stornoway	21.5

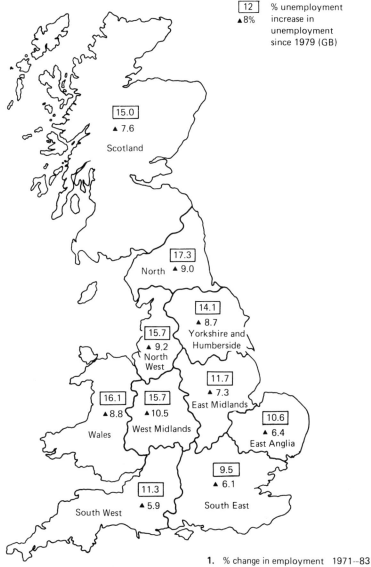

Key:

$\boxed{12}$ % unemployment
▲8% increase in unemployment since 1979 (GB)

Map values:

- Scotland: $\boxed{15.0}$ ▲ 7.6
- North: $\boxed{17.3}$ ▲ 9.0
- Yorkshire and Humberside: $\boxed{14.1}$ ▲ 8.7
- North West: $\boxed{15.7}$ ▲ 9.2
- East Midlands: $\boxed{11.7}$ ▲ 7.3
- Wales: $\boxed{16.1}$ ▲ 8.8
- West Midlands: $\boxed{15.7}$ ▲ 10.5
- East Anglia: $\boxed{10.6}$ ▲ 6.4
- South West: $\boxed{11.3}$ ▲ 5.9
- South East: $\boxed{9.5}$ ▲ 6.1

1. % change in employment 1971–83
2. by industrial sector 1979–83

	Agriculture, Forestry and Fishing	Coal, oil and natural gas	Electricity, gas + other energy and water supply	Metal manufacturing + ore and other mineral extraction	Chemicals + man-made fibres	Mechanical Engineering	Office Machinery, electrical engineering + instruments	Motor vehicles and parts	Other transport equipment	Other metal goods	Food, drink and tobacco	Textiles, leather footwear and clothing	Timber, wooden furniture, rubber, plastics etc.	Paper products, printing and publishing	Construction	Wholesale distribution and repair	Retail distribution	Hotels and catering	Transport	Postal services and telecommunications	Banking, Insurance, Finance	Public Administration etc.	Education	Medical and other health services	Other services
1	17▼	24▼	15▼	44▼	23▼	33▼	22▼	41▼	27▼	37▼	21▼	43▼	25▼	21▼	16▼	12▲	6▲	27▲	20▼	4▼	32▲	5▲	23▲	35▲	30▲
2	4▼	16▼	8▼	32▼	21▼	25▼	16▼	31▼	26▼	29▼	16▼	26▼	22▼	16▼	19▼	4▼	6▼	2▼	16▼	2▼	3▲	4▼	3▼	6▼	1▲

Source: **Employment Gazette** May 1984, Vol. 92, No. 5

NB figures rounded

Figure 4.2 The Geography of Employment Change 1979–83

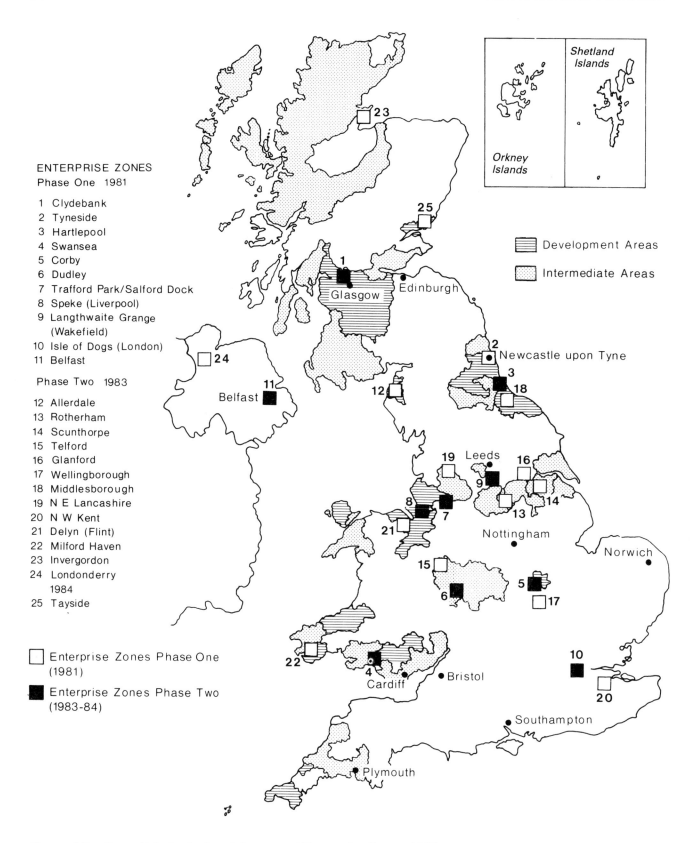

Figure 4.3   Great Britain Assisted Areas and Enterprise Zones 1985

actually created, and indeed, for bringing the wrong type of jobs to the wrong areas. Depressed peripheral regions, formerly heavily dependent upon heavy industries, now contracting, need employment diversification. The emphasis of regional policy upon capital investment has usually encouraged capital-intensive industry to move into such areas rather than the labour-intensive industries which would have broadened employment opportunities. Nevertheless, these policies have shifted jobs, even if nationally they have not created many. Until the 1970's, therefore, there was a general political consensus that some form of policy package for depressed regions could restore higher levels of employment, if only sufficient funding and commitment were available. In the event, many of the jobs that were shifted were principally via branch plant operations of both national and international concerns. So the effect of regional policies has been to add yet further vulnerability to what were already economically weak regions.

As unemployment rose in all regions the new 1979 Conservative government decided that a much more selective regional policy was required. As a result, although 'Areas for Expansion' as they are euphemistically called, still exist, their extent has been considerably reduced. Fig. 4.3 shows the relatively limited coverage of the designated areas, now restricted to the traditionally declining areas and those where special circumstances apply, such as the former iron and steel making area around Corby in Northants. Although some change of policy was probably desirable, the direction of the change signified a breakdown of the political consensus. On the left, greater state intervention has been advocated in the form of economic reflation and more direct assistance to industry. On the right,

government intervention has been seen as a retardant to economic growth, and the emphasis has been on freeing industry from the effects of bureaucracy. This approach is epitomised in the *Enterprise Zone* concept, originally conceived as a measure to provide employment and resuscitation for Britain's inner city areas. Operating rather in the same way as Freeports, the zones were to be free of the fettering effects of taxes, employment planning, pollution and welfare legislation. In the event, this proved too extreme to be politically acceptable and a modified version was introduced in 1980 and subsequently extended to other depressed areas outside the inner cities. Most legislation still applies within the zones, but as well as a measure of de-regulation, the emphasis seems to have switched back to one of enhanced financial assistance (Table 12). Economic growth is to be encouraged by a combination of financial incentives and streamlined planning controls, the latter to be identified by each local planning authority responsible. Apart from certain 'excluded uses' (e.g. hazardous substances, noisy production processes and, usually, large-scale retail developments) any development is allowed. The zones are intended to serve an ideological as well as a practical purpose, in demonstrating what can be achieved in a more 'laissez-faire' situation. 'Planning free' zones and 'Freeports' have also been proposed and are of the same spirit.

Apart from the Enterprise Zone policy there remain a bewildering array of specific government incentives, operated either directly by central departments, or indirectly via fringe bodies. An indication of their range is illustrated in Table 13a, which catalogues the variety of initiatives that apply in the county of Cleveland as a case example.

Table 12   The Enterprise Zone Package

— Exemption from Development Land Tax

— Exemption from rates on industrial and commercial property

— Possible 100% first year allowance for capital expenditures on industrial and commercial buildings against income and corporation tax

— Priority for treatment of applications (and some relaxation of certain criteria) for customs-free merchandising

— Exemption from Industrial Training Board levies and requests for information

— Reduction in government requests for information

— Greatly simplified planning regime (developments conforming with published schemes for zones do not require individual planning permission except 'Special Industrial Uses')

— Remaining controls will be speedily administered

Local Government

Local planning authorities have traditionally practised *industrial development planning* which involves, inter alia, the analysis of industrial structure and employment forecasting. When linked with demographic factors such as activity rates, housing demand, the need for shopping and other facilities, the land-use implications assume immense proportions. In the present arrangement, structure plans, as usual, provide the strategic policy framework, with local planning being concerned with implementation and providing the means of accommodating industrial development in specific areas. Preparing local plans involves surveying land availability and suitability, identifying sites for industrial estates and advance factories, and considering the adequacy of transportation infrastructure along with site service facilities. The plans are implemented in the usual way through the system of development control, or else by positive action by the local authority. This latter has now become much more widespread, and industrial development planning has now become subsumed within the much wider activity of *employment planning* which places less emphasis on land use considerations, but more on levels of employment.

Employment planning and job creation have now become a major pre-occupation of many local authorities, often taking precedence over conventional town and country planning, and involving purpose-designed teams of specialists drawn from a wide range of local authority functions, including planning. In those parts of the country where unemployment remains at a comparatively low level, and where growth is still occurring, town planners continue to perform conventional roles – analysing employment trends, making forecasts, formulating policies for the location of different types of industry and identifying sites – all with an emphasis on land use considerations. Where unemployment is at high levels these duties are still performed by planners, but the number of them, and their scope, has in many cases been drastically reduced. Committee structures have been changed, job descriptions have been rewritten and posts have disappeared as staff have been re-deployed in a concerted effort to induce economic regeneration and reduce unemployment.

The precise means which are open to local authorities in tackling this problem are rather limited, but have fallen under four headings

    land assembly
    advocacy
    (re)training
    direct assistance

i) Land assembly One of the major difficulties encountered by manufacturing industry in the older urban areas is the availability of vacant land. Land assembly is thus an appropriate and proper exercise in land use planning, and although simply making land available for manufacturing use is not going to create jobs automatically, it can be an important factor in retaining jobs by enabling existing firms to re-organise their plant. By making land available, properly provided with services, eg on an industrial estate, a local authority can at least enable industrial development to occur. Of course some authorities have easier access to land than others, and to appropriate funding. Thus the London borough of Hammersmith and Fulham, having access to Inner Area Partnership funds speculatively generated 1.5 m square feet of floorspace between 1978/9 and 1981/2.

ii) Advocacy Publicising an area's advantages is a familiar enough way to encourage outside investment, but many local authorities have found it necessary to engage in a much more sustained lobbying on behalf of particular industries and even individual firms than would have been imagined a generation ago. In Newcastle upon Tyne, for instance, where 80% of manufacturing jobs are concentrated in just 27 firms, principally in a limited industrial sector, the future not only of the shipbuilding industry but of individual firms is crucial to the city's economy, and the City Council have been vigorous in their advocacy on behalf of the city's interests, though with only limited success.

iii) Training The metropolitan districts, London boroughs and shire counties have wide powers in respect of education. An important option available therefore, is to engage in education and training programmes appropriate to the needs of modern manufacturing and service industries, particularly in Further Education. Thus Manchester City Council has identified three 'training objectives' specifically related to further education and retraining. They are intended to

– Enable the redistribution of the workforce by seeking to improve the access of the existing workforce or the unemployed to jobs
– Ensure that potential growth is not choked off by short term skill shortages
– Provide the unemployed and those with unsatisfying jobs with a means of enhancing their leisure, and enabling them to exploit better their own internal resources.

iv) Direct assistance Under Section 137 of the Local Government (Miscellaneous Provisions) Act, 1982, local authorities are explicitly enabled to spend the product of a 2p rate on financial assistance to commercial and industrial organisations, including loans, grants and guarantees. This is simply part of limited discretion for local authorities to act in the interests of their residents. Clearly, the product of a 2p rate means more in Westminster than in Whitehaven, but it is a useful source of funds which have been applied in a great variety of ways, but especially by means of an *Enterprise Board*. These are public sector development capital companies which can provide pump-priming investment in local firms. The West Midlands Enterprise Board, for instance, reckons that over 1500 jobs have been created or saved by its activities, and its investments in various firms now stand at £3.5m.

Cleveland County Council offers a useful example of the type of changes taking place. Unemployment levels of over 20% have forced the council to take a fresh look at its policy-making and organisation in order to give greater emphasis to economic regeneration. In addition to aid from central sources and the EEC, the county council has sought to identify initiatives, often in partnership with the private sector (Table 13). In 1983 the following priorities were established prior to completing a deliberately delayed review of the Structure Plan:

- investigation of new economic initiatives and implementation of agreed projects
- adaptation of procedures for monitoring structure and local plans to ensure that economic information and analysis is available in forms that relate directly to the assessment of economic initiatives while continuing to inform on other aspects of the plan
- provision of design and advisory services to other county departments, borough councils and other public agencies on landscape matters, conservation, development control, local plans, and technical services etc.

Among the district authorities, land use planning has retained much more of its traditional role, due to the immediacy of the planning function at this level. Nevertheless, the majority of county districts, particularly in the metropolitan areas where the recession has hit hardest, are now making changes to their organisation and practice similar to those noted at county level earlier. A 1982 survey by the Association of District Councils, covering 75% of their membership, revealed that 87% of the respondents were engaged in forms of industrial

development and promotion, with 15% having established enterprise trusts in their area and 11% having set up co-operatives to help small companies market their products and pool their resources. 41% had embarked upon joint ventures with the private sector and 34% with other public sector bodies. 16% had given grants to local firms, and 18% had made loans. 82% had provided sites and 51% actual industrial and commercial premises. By such means, therefore, local government has found itself in a much more responsive role than it would have been possible to imagine in the early 1960's, with planning's function modified and in these respects made much more interactive with the private sector.

4.3 CONCLUSION

Because of the changing circumstances into which planning has moved since the mid 1970's, it is difficult to assess the success of the new measures and approaches that have been adopted. The faith of central government in small firms – the supposed seed-bed of recovery – and in the freeing of the private sector from state intervention has yet to be proved one way or the other. There are fears in some quarters that Enterprise Zones merely shift job opportunities from one area to another, just as did the former regional policy. Moreover, some evidence is emerging to suggest that the zones are no more effective at creating jobs and encouraging expansion than natural market forces. For the majority of firms, the only benefits are often rate exemption and tax relief, with few of the remaining perks actually utilised. Central government's role, however, is clearly of fundamental importance, for it can make such major changes in the economy as modifying the shape and nature of the work force by adopting lower retirement ages or raising the school-leaving age, or encouraging concepts such as work sharing with its consequential change in attitude towards work and leisure. Only central government, too, can adopt regional policies of some kind, although clearly the EEC has some part to play in this. Given the complicated nature of the problem, it is not surprising that government initiatives, whether directly or by way of fringe bodies, or through their relationships with local government, should appear Byzantine in complexity. As a result of the myriad schemes that are available and the variety of different agencies at work, it is equally unsurprising that many firms are unaware of all the benefits to which they may be entitled. Equally, the spatial jig-saw within which the various bodies operate, ranging from rural areas (CoSIRA) to the inner cities (Urban Programme) by way of the Assisted Areas, adds to the confusion, and raises the question as to the

Section A   Financial incentives available from outside sources

REGIONAL DEVELOPMENT GRANTS   From 1st August 1982, new machinery, plant, buildings and works — 22% of capital costs in Special Development Area

SELECTIVE FINANCIAL ASSISTANCE (Section 7 Finance)   Grants towards the costs of industrial and commercial projects

ASSISTANCE TO SERVICE INDUSTRY   For offices, research and development units and other service industry undertakings a fixed grant of £2,000 for each employee moving with his work, up to a 30% limit, and an additional grant of up to £8,000 for each job created

ADVANCE FACTORIES, NURSERY UNITS & WORKSHOPS   Under certain special circumstances rent-free periods may be considered for a standard advance factory which can be rented on terms in accordance with modern estate management principles.   In cases where tenants require bespoke factories or wish to purchase on long lease basis, mortgages can be arranged through English Industrial Estates

TAX ALLOWANCES   Normal tax allowances for buildings, plant and machinery are unaffected by regional grants

FINANCE FROM EUROPEAN COMMUNITY FUNDS   Loans may be available on favourable terms from the European Investment Bank and the European Coal and Steel Community

IN-PLANT TRAINING SCHEMES   Grants to assist firms with expansion projects to train employees in necessary skills

FINANCE FOR TOURISM PROJECTS   Grants or loans available for selected tourist projects from the Regional Tourist Board and CoSIRA

SECTION 8 1972 INDUSTRY ACT   Grants and loans for certain industries to improve productivity and efficiency under National Selective Assistance and Sectoral Industry Schemes

PRODUCT AND PROCESS DEVELOPMENT SCHEME   Grants towards costs of new products or processes

GOVERNMENT LOAN GUARANTEE SCHEME   Government guaranteed loans of up to £75,000

ASSISTANCE FROM CoSIRA   Loans for small industries and tourism in rural areas

GRANTS FOR TRANSPORT FACILITIES   Provision of rail and road facilities

BRITISH OVERSEAS TRADE BOARD ASSISTANCE TO EXPORTERS   Schemes designed to aid exporters

BRITISH TECHNOLOGY GROUP ASSISTANCE   Finance for innovative industry

CONTRACT PREFERENCE SCHEME   This scheme affords preference, other considerations being equal, to firms from Special Development Areas and Development Areas tendering for Government contracts

DEPARTMENT OF EMPLOYMENT ASSISTANCE   Assistance with recruitment to relocating and expanding companies

BRITISH STEEL CORPORATION (INDUSTRY) LTD   Grants are available towards the cost of consultancy studies or of research and development.   Less frequently equity funds may be available for steel-related enterprises while management skills and advice are readily available together with expert assistance in obtaining land and buildings

ENTERPRISE ZONE STATUS   Tax concessions, capital allowances and other exemptions within the Hartlepool Enterprise Zone

DERELICT LAND RECLAMATION SCHEME   Grants for effecting reclamation and development of derelict land

Section B   Local Authority Initiatives

DIRECT ASSISTANCE TO INDUSTRY
—Local purchasing by the council
—Use of superannuation fund for investment purposes
—Selection of capital projects on basis of employment consequences
—Cleveland Assistance Scheme for Employment (CASE) — to encourage small and medium-sized firms to recruit additional permanent employees by providing a 6-month subsidy
—Flexible Assistance Scheme — to permit council to step in and sieze on any opportunity to reduce unemployment or to regenerate local economy e.g. by providing finance, services or facilities
—Small business grant/loan — financial assistance to encourage small firms to create and maintain jobs
—Encouragement and support for industrial and service co-operatives
—Provision of industrial mortgages
—Expanded and improved promotion for Cleveland
—Other incentives — new business competition, invention fund, Information Bulletin, Science and Technology Fair, links with Teesside Polytechnic, Business and Technology Centre

MSC AND OTHER TRAINING SCHEMES
—Extension of existing schemes — especially for environmental work
—Examination of possibilities for new schemes
—Develop industry for community benefit e.g. joinery, welding, production of overalls, etc.
—Establish information technology centre to give young unemployed training and work experience in micro-electronics and information technology

INDUSTRIAL SITES/PREMISES/INFRA-STRUCTURE
—Survey of availability and suitability
—Reclamation/redevelopment of industrial sites
—Access improvements
—Services and premises provision
—Environmental improvements

DEVELOPMENT OF TOURISM AND RECREATIONAL ACTIVITY

COMMUNITY EMPLOYMENT INITIATIVES
—Promotion of schemes for economic activity involving close co-operation of voluntary groups, local authorities and other local organisations within communities
—Appointment of community employment development officers in five areas of high unemployment — to promote schemes and ensure maximum take-up of initiatives, ensure co-ordination of local organisations and services to meet needs of long-term unemployed within communities, and to provide advice on skill development and training opportunities
—Wherever possible to influence demand for jobs by encouraging early retirement, job sharing, increased education/training, migration, reduction of overtime etc
—Improved economic information, analysis and monitoring
—Improved working arrangements within county council and with industry and commerce
—Establishment of an Enterprise Board to provide equity and loan finance to local firms.

Source: Cleveland County Council, 1983.
Note: Amounts and availability of grants change from time to time.

Table 13   Employment initiatives and Cleveland County Council

degree of compatability between their various aims and objectives, and indeed, the extent to which their effort may be duplicated. While physical planning matters are the province of the DOE, assistance to the Designated Areas (ie Regional Policy) is the province of the Department of Trade and Industry.

While local government has been taking a much more active interest in economic performance, it has done so rather hesitantly since there is no statutory obligation for a local authority to assist the local economy, and no suggestion as to what sort of obligation should be discharged at county or district level. It is by no means clear whether the local authorities are simply engaging in local first aid, or whether they are beginning to engage in full blown economic planning. Some county authorities, especially in metropolitan areas undoubtedly aspire to the latter, but the great majority would admit that they can only attempt the former. The structure planning process clearly offers the opportunity for some kind of integrated economic planning, yet without national guidelines, it is not surprising that DOE pressure has encouraged a backing-off from such an approach. In many counties, structure plan review and monitoring procedures have been relegated in priority in favour of a more ad hoc attack on immediate problems.

At district level, in contrast to most other areas of planning, those planners involved in employment matters are attempting to get to grips with the development industry. Informal plans and planning briefs look set to play an increasing role in the future, given their accent on responsiveness and flexibility. The more formal planning procedures will continue to play a vital role in environmental protection, especially where green-field sites are concerned, but the need for speed in handling applications, especially where jobs are concerned has become paramount.

All of this activity may yet be constrained by the persistent pressure being exerted by central government on local authorities to restrain their spending. In this light, it is hard to imagine local government being allowed its head in economic planning, even if it was uniformly of a political complexion to prefer to do so. Such activity, in conjunction with the private sector smack too much of the 'local state' to be palatable in either Whitehall or Westminster.

Further reading

A R Townsend 1983 provides a fascinating and detailed account of the extent and depth of recession in U.K. industry in *The Impact of Recession* (Croom Helm). See also J B Goddard & A G Champion 1983 *The Urban and Regional Transformation of Britain* (Methuen) for a succinct account in Chapter 1 of overall structural change. For a good introduction to right wing employment policies and especially Enterprise Zones see R Botham and G Lloyd (1983) The political economy of Enterprise Zones, *National Westminster Bank Quarterly Review* (May). For a similar treatment of employment changes see A Fox 1984 Employment trends in Britain and the USA, *Barclays Bank Quarterly Review* (May). For an evaluation of Enterprise Zones see M G Lloyd in *The Planner* (June 1984).

For employment re-generation see the special edition of *The Planner* (Sept/Oct 1983). More general treatment will be found in S Fothergill and G Gudgin (1982) *Unequal growth, Urban and Regional Employment Change in the UK* (Heineman) and in D Massey & R Meegan 1982 *The Anatomy of Job Loss: the how, why and where of employment decline* (Methuen). The monthly journal of the Department of Employment, *The Employment Gazette* is a good source of current employment statistics.

CHAPTER 5
LEISURE

One of the aspirations of the Garden City movement was to integrate opportunities for work and leisure. Such an aspiration has greater relevance today, given the increased opportunity for leisure as 'work' activities have contracted. In addition, of course, the rise in demand for leisure has increased opportunities for employment in leisure-related industries which have now become important sources of jobs, and through international tourism figured increasingly in the balance of trade. Central government, fringe bodies and both major tiers of local government engage in both employment planning and in planning for leisure, but there has so far been little co-ordination between the two fields, nor between the various agencies at work within each. It is not easy to assign a precise role for town and country planners in either field, nor to disentangle their activities from those of other departments. Thus, many leisure facilities may relate to the education and health services, while the planning of employment is likely to have more to do with the characteristics of the local labour force than with land use, and may be barely related to the system of public administration at all. Both activities, of course, are dominated by the private sector, and in reality while both central and local government are widely involved, their capacity for precise planning is limited, even though town and country planners are active in both fields.

5.1 ATTITUDES TO LEISURE AND PATTERNS OF ACTIVITY

The involvement of public administration in the field of leisure has a longer history, in local government at least, than that of employment planning. It stems from a series of value judgements about leisure which, while they may reflect Victorian attitudes still form part of the received wisdom on what is currently undertaken by public bodies. We can formulate these judgements as three principles:

– for the sake of public order, premises involved in the sale of alcohol, or offering public performance should be licensed
– self-improvement should be promoted through the provision of such facilities as libraries, museums, galleries, the subsidisation of the arts and the provision of adult education
– personal fitness should be encouraged by the provision of facilities for sports and open-air activities of both a formal kind requiring playing fields etc., or of an informal kind requiring public open space or access to the countryside.

These attitudes reveal leisure as a peripheral activity, but increasingly this notion is being challenged, and leisure is being seen as a valid activity in its own right and of equal worth as work. These shifts in social attitudes towards leisure have been initiated by the changing relations between 'work' and 'spare time' activities, underlain by increasing levels of personal affluence. The reduction of the working week and increase in holiday entitlement is indicated in Fig 5.1. Greater amounts of disposable income and expenditure on leisure related goods are additional features of the change that has taken place in British lifestyles since the 1950's. All these influences have widened the scope of leisure pursuits and facilitated much higher levels of participation than was the case previously. Home based activities (gardening, DIY, TV and Hi-Fi), informal outdoor activities (day trips and visits, picnics and barbecues etc), active sports, adult education, cultural pastimes and holidays away from home, have all increased dramatically.

Leisure is therefore being made more accessible than ever before to a wider range of a more mobile public with more free time. In consequence, the provision of facilities where needed by public and private sector alike, to meet or encourage demand, can present problems of compatability with other activities expressed in terms of land use conflict and competition.

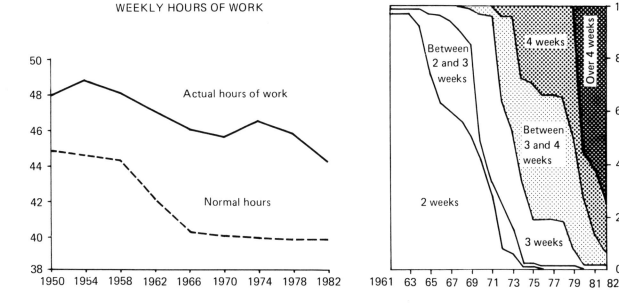

Source: **Social Trends** HMSO

Figure 5.1   Hours of work and holiday entitlement for UK manual employees

5.2   PLANNING AND LEISURE

Despite the proliferation of fringe bodies, and the extensive ramification of the interests of central government, the majority of public sector activity in leisure planning and provision is in the hands of local government. Although the fringe bodies, for instance, have extensive research and advisory functions, their combined budgets are only c 5% of those devoted to leisure by local government, if we include those leisure activities which are funded by the education, welfare and social services. Unfortunately, even local government activity is complicated since much of it is of a discretionary rather than a mandatory kind, so the involvement of any one local authority depends more upon local enthusiasm than central direction. In general, the largest urban authorities with large, integrated leisure services departments are more active than small rural authorities, although the extent to which an authority contains a resort or major tourist attraction is clearly important. Conventionally, a distinction is made between tourism and recreation, on the basis that tourism activities turn upon overnight stays, but, of course, tourists use facilities designed for the recreation of local residents, and vice versa. To simplify a complex field, we can identify the planning process in leisure as relating to three components: monitoring, regulation, and actual provision, performed by three types of agency:

central government, fringe bodies and local authorities. A summary of agency responsibilities and activities is provided in Table 14.

Monitoring and Research

Although monitoring and research into leisure activities is carried out to some degree by virtually every government organisation involved, this function is especially the responsibility of the fringe bodies and of local government. In strictly land use planning terms, the operation of the *Countryside Commission* has been easily the most influential in rural areas, through its research and development function, undertaking experimental projects, and offering advice and grant aid to local authorities. Reference is made in Chapter 8 to some of the activities of the Commission, which is specifically charged 'to keep under review all matters relating to the enjoyment of the countryside, its conservation and enhancement and the need to secure public access for the purpose of open air recreation, and to consult with local authorities in these matters'. In urban areas the *Sports Council* and the *Regional Councils for Sport and Recreation* (answerable jointly to the Sports Council and the Countryside Commission) have been perhaps the most influential, for in addition to the grant aid function of the Sports Council, the Regional Councils are charged with a liaison, information and

Table 14   Planning for leisure

AGENCY	RESPONSIBILITY	PROVISION
CENTRAL GOVERNMENT		
Department of Environment	Town and country planning, local authorities, inner city partnership, rural development, sport, outdoor recreation, water-based recreation	Grant-aid to local authorities, fringe bodies & to voluntary bodies. Designation of cherished lands etc.
Department of Education and Science	Arts, museums, adult education, community service	Grant aid to local authorities and to fringe bodies
Home Office	Licensing, Urban Aid Programme	Grant aid to local authorities etc.
Department of Trade and Industry	Tourism	Grant aid to local authorities etc.
Department of Health and Social Security	Hospitals, health and social services	Grant aid to local authorities etc.
FRINGE BODIES		
British Waterways Board	Inland navigation	Maintenance of waterways
British Tourist Authority	Tourism	Grant aid to Tourist Boards & thus to private sector
Forestry Commission	Woodlands	Forest-based recreation facilities
Regional Water Authorities	Reservoirs	Water-based recreation facilities
Arts Council	Arts and cultural activities	Grant aid to Regional Arts Councils & to individual enterprises
Sports Council	Sport & physical recreation	Grant aid to Regional Councils for sport & recreation
Countryside Commission	Countryside recreation	Grant aid to local authorities & National Park Committees
Development Commission	Social aspects of rural development	Grant aid to local authorities etc.
National Council for Social Services	Social and voluntary provision	Grant aid to local authorities & to voluntary bodies, community associations
LOCAL AUTHORITIES		
Metropolitan Counties	Structure planning, transport planning, cultural activities, caravan sites, participation in regional recreation strategies	Museums and galleries, country parks, footpaths, archaeology & archives, scenic routes, subsidies to regional arts associations & to individual enterprises, misc. facilities
Non-metropolitan Counties	As above	As above plus adult education and education-linked sports and cultural facilities
Metropolitan Districts	Local planning, Education, Social Services, Recreation	Playing fields, sports centres, libraries, museums, parks & open spaces, cultural & recreational promotions, adult education & education-linked facilities
Non-Metropolitan Districts	Local planning, Social Services, Recreation	As above except for educational activities
Parish Councils	Responsibility for facilities provided	Parks, swimming pools, bridleways, footpaths, seats & shelters (Under agency from district/council or by precept in their own right)

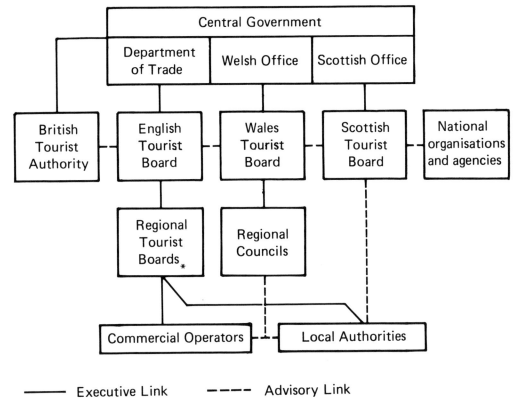

——— Executive Link   – – – Advisory Link

*   Regional Tourist Boards

Northumbria	East Anglia
Cumbria	Thames and Chilterns
North West	West Country
Yorkshire & Humberside	London
Heart of England	Southern
East Midlands	South East

Source: Planning for Tourism in England, Planning Advisory
Note 1 (1981) English Tourist Board

Figure 5.2   The Tourist Board framework

co-ordination function. While this may be regarded as a hope rather than a rigorously applied principle, because of the great variety of ways in which local authorities undertake leisure activities and the enormous proliferation of private sector leisure outlets, this function is nevertheless of particular importance given the regional scale at which recreation may be practised, and the need for regional strategies against which local authorities and others can plan their own developments.

Under the 1969 Development of Tourism Act, the *British Tourist Authority* was established to supervise strategic planning for tourism in Britain, along with three national *Tourist Boards*. Although the Boards have a promotional role relating to the marketing of facilities and the improvement of tourist amenities, these functions clearly have town and country planning implications when translated into specific activities. Grant aid to provide overnight accommodation, for instance, has obvious repercussions on existing residential provision, matters of access, parking and general amenity. Within the national organisation, the English Tourist Board has set up a structure of twelve *regional tourist boards* to achieve co-ordination and co-operation on tourism issues between local authorities and private operators at the regional level. Fig 5.2 sets out the framework of Tourist Board operations as well as illustrating the existence of executive and advisory links. Tourism strategies are presented for each region, and a contribution is usually made by the boards to the structure planning process.

Monitoring and research at local government level has been mainly through the medium of the local planning authority. Often in conjunction with the Countryside Commission, local planning authorities have drawn up inventories of leisure facilities, and undertaken capacity studies especially with regard to recreational 'honey pots' in rural areas. Subject plans may be produced on aspects of leisure provision and there is coverage in most of the county structure plans.

Regulation

Within the framework of central government statutes, and the advice offered by fringe bodies, the regulation of leisure activities is overwhelmingly the province of local authorities. The licensing of activities referred to earlier is undertaken by the local magistracy. The formal method of planning control, of course, is through the granting or withholding of planning permission. At least in theory, planning authorities have the means of controlling new developments and restricting those which might impair their policies relating to leisure provision. Most commercial leisure facilities require not only planning permission, but public notification and so the planning authority has every opportunity to keep in close touch with new pressures such as the recent expansion of 'leisure centres' (effectively amusement arcades) from the seafront to the high street of every provincial town.

In a different vein, the application of conservation policies in both urban and rural areas outlined in Chapter 8 is very relevant to leisure activities. The designation of National Parks, Areas of Outstanding Natural Beauty, or Heritage Coasts, the application of Conservation Area policies, and the listing of buildings of architectural and historic interest have implications for leisure activities as well as more general amenity considerations. In a less formal way, local planning authori-

ties could be said to be exercising 'regulation' by the development of Country Parks, Scenic Routes, and negotiating access and management agreements. The idea of country parks was promoted in the 1968 Countryside Act as a means of promoting and developing facilities for informal recreation in countryside close to urban areas and so diverting visitor pressure from more popular and increasingly sensitive remote rural areas. Equally, the designation of scenic routes encourages the use of certain rural roads to relieve congestion on others. By such means the movement of people for the purposes of informal recreation are being managed, if not strictly controlled.

Provision

Leisure provision is dominated by the private sector but local authorities virtually monopolise the public sector provision of leisure facilities. Of all the areas of public sector leisure expenditure listed in Fig 5.3, the provision of public parks, open spaces, sports facilities and playing fields are of special importance from a land use point of view because of their extensive demands for space. In this regard, local authorities were urged first in 1964 by a joint circular from the DES and the then Ministry of Housing and Local Government, and then in 1972 by the Cobham Report, to consider how the leisure needs of local communities could best be met by utilising the facilities provided in education programmes. This has not just been a matter of throwing open school playing fields to more general use (and still insufficiently offered), but in several local authority areas, following the revolutionary policy initiated in Cambridgeshire as early as the 1930s, deliberate use has been made of school premises as a whole community resource. This has been most easily achieved where the re-organisation of secondary education has led to new school building programmes. Such new schools can be more easily purpose-designed for use as 'community colleges', with joint school and community use of playing fields, swimming pools, drama studios and concert halls, with specialist classrooms available for the purposes of adult education as well as for normal school purposes. Such developments are unevenly spread, however, as local authorities have varied in their response to this suggestion, not only by preference but also by virtue of the physical practicability of achieving such ends. (It may be worth noting, incidentally, that the provision of library services and adult education classes are the only leisure services that local authorities are *obliged* to provide.) Specific provision of other activities is mainly a matter of local tradition and prefer-

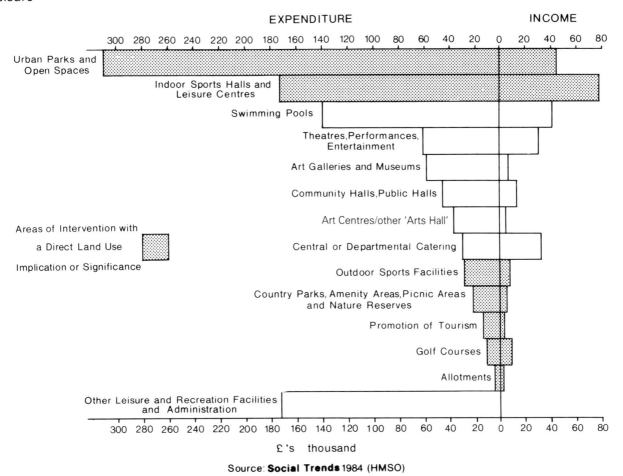

Figure 5.3 Local authority expenditure and income on Leisure and Recreation 1982–83 (England and Wales)

ence. In general, what has been inherited from the past continues to be supported, simply because the withdrawal of facilities, especially in urban areas, is often politically unacceptable. Beyond this, of course, the changing availability of grant aid from central government and fringe bodies plays an important part in policy relating to new developments.

By its nature, though, much of planning is future-oriented and so its operation is less concerned with present activities as with creating the best conditions for enabling future development to occur in the most appropriate manner. An example of this contextual approach is that of the Lothian Regional Council in Scotland. Its Leisure Services Department, formed in 1975, published the results of a five year study in 1982 in the form of a three volume leisure strategy relating to urban, rural and arts-based recreation (Table 15). The strategy identified location as the key issue in attaining satisfactory levels of use, emphasising the need for provision to be related to the pattern of population density.

A second key issue was the need to ensure that access to leisure activities was available to all social groups, and not just to the affluent, car-borne sections of the population. This implied a certain positive discrimination in favour of certain areas. As these two issues combine together across the three policy sectors they demonstrated how future investment could best match existing provision and produce a spatial distribution of opportunity appropriate to the social needs of the population. Although in this instance the impetus lay with the Leisure Services Department, the development control powers of the local planning authority will contribute the means of implementation.

5.3 CONCLUSION

Of the three components identified in the leisure planning process, the local planning authority seems best placed to undertake the monitoring function. While the

URBAN RECREATIONAL STRATEGY

to increase participation among those groups who traditionally remain inactive

to provide a range of recreation opportunities for all sections of the community

to optimise the use of facilities

to provide new facilities

to encourage individual achievement in sport

COUNTRYSIDE RECREATIONAL STRATEGY

to balance recreation development with conservation of countryside resources

to stimulate increased participation

to encourage development of facilities

to foster a wider knowledge of the countryside

ARTS STRATEGY

to increase awareness of the arts

to ensure an even geographical distribution of the informal arts

to support the formal arts

to encourage creativity and variety

to encourage higher standards

Source: Lothian Regional Council
Recreation Strategy 1982

Table 15   Lothian Regional Council Leisure Strategy

monitoring of informal recreation has received a fair amount of attention in rural areas, much more work remains to be done in urban areas, where the provision of public sector facilities in particular often owes more to the energies and ambitions of the constituent former authorities, sometimes stretching back over a century, than of rational planning in the 1980's. Even many of the new multi-purpose sports centres built in the 1970's were either the last throw of the old authorities or dashing symbols of vigour on the part of the new, rather than the result of a careful assessment of local needs. Further, the benefits and disbenefits of tourism have not been sufficiently monitored by local authorities, except in places with high tourist activity. Only recently have many local authorities woken up to the fact that leisure is a job producing activity as well as a pastime for local residents and visitors. Although there are difficulties relating to seasonality and low pay, the promotion of tourism and the development of leisure facilities is a legitimate part of a local authority's activities and could form a useful part of a job-creation strategy. It has been shown that almost 50% of tourist income can be retained in a local economy, while facilities available for local residents can be enhanced by the tapping of the tourist market. Thus, the recognition of visitor pressure at the Ironbridge Gorge industrial museum complex in Shropshire has led to private investment in a country club and hotel facility at Telford. This has provided local residents with additional jobs along with sports and recreational facilities which would otherwise not have been available. Similarly, the monitoring of tourist

activity at Windsor revealed that few visitors either stayed long or spent much in one of Britain's major tourist towns. Visitors were, therefore, a pressure on local resources, rather than a resource to be utilised. It was consequently suggested that the provision of further leisure facilities and additional hotel accommodation would enable the tourist market to be tapped more effectively. As long as these facilities were provided with appropriate reference to the other needs of the town – an essential planning function – then there would be obvious benefits to the local community. Such exercises are entirely appropriate to a system of town and country planning searching for a clear role in leisure matters, and can be easily accommodated within the existing concept of local implementation of county structure planning.

Further reading

A J Veal 1975 *Recreation Planning and Management in the New Local Government Authorities* (University of Birmingham) is good introduction to local authority activities, along with a regional study from the same source, J White & M C Dunn 1975 *Countryside Recreation Planning and Prospects in the W Midlands.* J A Patmore 1983 *Recreation and Planning* (Blackwell) and M Shoard 1980 *The Theft of the Countryside* (M T Smith) are key texts on recreation in rural areas generally. A critique of urban sports provision is provided by M Hillman & A Whalley 1977 *Fair Play for all* (PEP).

A useful historical perspective on tourism planning will be found in J Heeley 1981 Planning for tourism in Britain, *Town Planning Review* 52 pp 61–71, while the English Tourist Board's Planning for tourism in England, *Planning Advisory Note* of 1983 is a good current guide. For the best general introduction to leisure statistics see *Social Trends* published annually by HMSO. The monthly publication of the English Tourist Board's *Tourism in Action* contains useful information on different local authority tourism initiatives.

CHAPTER 6
TRANSPORTATION

Insofar as town and country planning is about the zoning of land uses and the location of particular activities, it is also about the need for transportation, since goods and persons need to move between areas in different land use. Conversely, any system of transportation itself helps to determine the types of land uses that are practicable at any location. The complex of relationships between land use and transportation was studied in several major cities and regions over the 1960's and 1970's and its subtleties have been the basis of whole books rather than short chapters. In this chapter, therefore, our objective is not to reduce to absurdly simple terms that which is exceedingly complex, but rather to identify the role filled by the planner and to point to some of the major issues faced by the profession. Transportation in the context of planning is customarily viewed in terms of the different ways of moving goods and persons, and the implications they have for the objectives of land use planning, but social and economic impact must also be considered alongside.

6.1   TRANSPORT TRENDS

The changes that have taken place in transport since 1945 and their impact on society have been dramatic. Inland waterways have predominantly become a recreational facility, the railway network has been drastically reduced and its proportion of goods traffic slashed, while road transport has increased in volume and extent. The obvious mark of this change is the massive increase in vehicle numbers, with car ownership itself increasing by 676% between 1950–81 (see Table 16). The size and number of heavy goods vehicles has also increased, while the expansion of coach traffic, especially since de-regulation in 1981, is simply another sign of the increased efficiency of long distance road travel. This efficiency has been brought about not only by advances in vehicle design, but also by an extensive road building and improvement programme which has been the subject of considerable planning activity and controversy.

British cities became increasingly congested in the 1950's due to their inability to absorb the higher levels of private car ownership. In 1963 the Buchanan Report (Traffic in Towns) signalled government recognition of the problem and recommended comprehensive redevelopment of cities in order to accommodate the motor car, subject to certain environmental and cost constraints. Design standards were put forward which included vehicular-pedestrian segregation and networks of urban motorways to facilitate the movement of through traffic and to provide for local access. Essentially these were engineering solutions but of course motorway development schemes of various kinds were the order of the day in the later 1950's and early 1960's, as is shown in Table 16.

Most major urban areas have some legacy to show from this period of extensive civil engineering, even if only fragments of an incomplete scheme, abandoned as attitudes changed and the money ran out in the later 1960's and early 1970's. By this time, the adverse environmental impact of such schemes had provoked a backlash of public opinion against them. Few road proposals, whether they were inter or intra urban escaped without an extensive public inquiry, usually focussing on the alignment of by-passes and motorways. In consequence, the emphasis in transportation planning switched from major engineering works to more modest traffic management schemes utilising existing road systems. Again, most towns bear witness to this policy shift by their ubiquitous one-way systems, traffic restrictions, parking policies and pedestrianised streets.

These various transport changes have had a variable impact upon the public. As is shown in Fig 6.1, while there has been a 27% increase in private transport passenger kilometres since 1964, public transport by bus or coach has suffered a reduction of 58%. Yet 39% of all households in Britain still do not have regular use of a car, and in parts of the northern regions this figure is much higher (49% in Scotland). This group contains not only those barred from car ownership by age or income, but also those who are incapable of using any kind of

Table 16   Transport Statistics: Great Britain 1982

	Trunk Roads	Classified Principal Roads 1	Classified Non-principal Roads 2	Unclassified Roads	Motorways 3	Local Authority Motorways 4	All Surfaced Roads	Motor Vehicles Currently Licensed ('000) Private Cars & Vans	Motor Vehicles Currently Licensed ('000) All Vehicles	Vehicles per km of Road
1964	13,885	31,902	107,205	157,845	460	10	310,887	8,247	12,370	40
1965	13,986	31,950	107,245	159,765	558	13	312,946	8,917	12,938	41
1966	14,936	32,049	107,237	161,301	621	10	314,623	9,513	13,286	42
1967	14,162	32,531	107,243	161,666	750	11	315,602	10,303	14,096	45
1968	14,370	32,504	107,250	163,565	890	16	317,689	10,816	14,447	45
1969	14,439	32,533	107,254	166,089	946	18	320,315	11,227	14,751	46
1970	14,463	32,584	107,285	168,152	1,022	35	322,484	11,515	14,950	46
1971	14,662	32,737	107,388	169,872	1,235	35	324,659	12,062	15,478	48
1972	15,049	32,825	107,404	172,428	1,609	60	327,706	12,717	16,117	49
1973	15,034	32,813	107,186	172,159	1,676	64	327,191	13,497	17,014	52
1974	15,128	32,840	107,564	173,455	1,793	85	328,987	13,639	17,252	52
1975	15,250	32,912	107,687	174,101	1,894	86	329,950	13,747	17,501	53
1976	15,480	33,218	107,855	176,277	2,084	88	332,831	14,047	17,832	54
1977	15,241	33,594	108,121	177,726	2,156	99	334,682	N.A.	N.A.	—
1978	14,825	34,199	108,534	178,674	2,283	110	336,233	14,069	17,772	53
1979	14,813	34,438	108,574	180,023	2,341	116	337,348	14,568	18,625	55
1980	14,844	34,306	109,001	181,317	2,444	118	339,467	15,073	19,210	57
1981	14,895	34,545	108,716	183,569	2,524	104	341,724	15,267	19,355	57
1982	14,885	34,584	108,878	184,473	2,560	99	343,320	15,687	19,770	58

1   Class 1 roads prior to 1967
2   Class 2 and Class 3 roads prior to 1967
3   Included in trunk roads
4   Included in classified principal roads
5   Unclassified roads include an estimate for England
All road lengths in kilometers   N.A. – not available.

Source: Based on data from Transport Statistics: Great Britain 1964–74, 1972 – 1982, HMSO

NB data 1973–82 not strictly comparable with that for 1964–72 due to change in recording method.

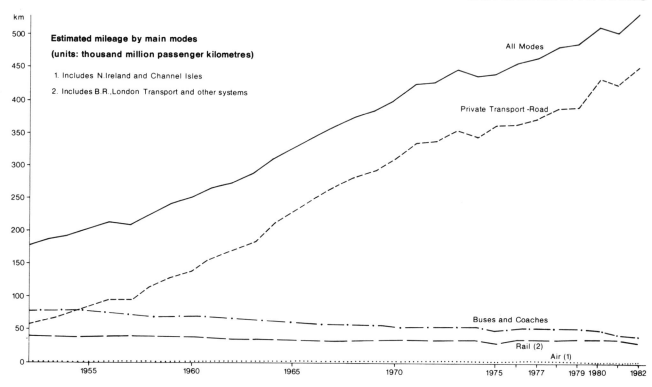

Figure 6.1   Passenger Transport in Great Britain 1952–1982

transport by infirmity or disability. Even car ownership is no guarantee of mobility of course, for while the family car is being used, say, by one member of the family for travel to work, it cannot be used by others. In the absence of public transport these persons are rendered immobile. This has had the severest implications in rural areas, and the more remote, the more severe. Even densely populated areas, though, have not escaped reductions in public transport services and increases in costs.

In a similar fashion, the human as well as financial costs of new road construction have been borne unequally by different sections of the community, with the inner urban areas being the hardest hit. Apart from the breakdown of social and friendship ties caused by demolition to make way for new and improved roads, there is also the severance of those neighbourhoods remaining. Many of those who live near new roads have seen property values decline as levels of pollution, noise and vibration have risen. This often sets in train further social dislocation as those most able to move to alternative locations do so. In consequence, while these various trends have favoured the personal mobility of the more affluent, the costs have been borne, in general, by the more disadvantaged in the community,

neatly illustrating once again the social consequences of technical solutions to planning problems.

While in modal terms air transport within Britain is relatively insignificant, proposals to build new or extend existing airports have consistently engendered considerable debate. This has often involved lengthy public inquiries where the matter is effectively taken out of the hands of the local planning authority and given over to the Secretary of State. In particular, of course, policy for the Third London Airport has still to be finalised.

6.2 TRANSPORT POLICY AND CENTRAL GOVERNMENT

The essential nature of transport has made it an important topic of public concern and debate into which the government is drawn inevitably. Government intervention is on both economic and environmental grounds and takes two main forms. First there are general national policies towards such matters as economic growth, regional development and energy, where transport is an essential component. Secondly, there are policies directed specifically towards transport and its sub sectors including financial support for particular manufacturing industries and strategies for road, rail, air, ports and shipping.

The major central department responsible for the co-ordination of these policies is the Department of Transport, which has four separate functions:

- regulation of private transport by legislation in the interests of safety and the environment (eg lead in petrol, safety belts, driver and vehicle testing etc)
- allocation of funds to county councils in England following consideration of submitted expenditure plans
- supervision of British Railways Board, National Bus Company and the British Transport Docks Board
- building and maintenance of motorways and major trunk roads in England.

The Scottish and Welsh Offices perform similar duties for their areas. The licensing of bus services, fares, crews and vehicles is the responsibility of eleven regional bodies of Traffic Commissioners who act as independent watchdogs.

It would be a mistake, however, to believe that the Department of Transport has been the seat of a rational national transport planning policy. As with so much of government activity, transport policies have evolved almost by default and principally in response to particular crises. A combination of socio-economic conditions, the influence of pressure groups and academic opinion have tended to make particular packages of policy the accepted wisdom of the time. Thus the high traffic forecasts of the 1960's combined with relative affluence, the popularity of redevelopment and the influence of the road lobby all combined to favour a period of extensive civil engineering solutions to traffic problems. In the 1970's, economic decline, cutbacks in public expenditure, a preference for rehabilitation and an influential environmental lobby prompted a policy reversal. The Department of Transport is, nevertheless, an important actor since it determines the outlines of policy within which local government activities are approved.

6.3 TRANSPORT PLANNING AND LOCAL GOVERNMENT

Since the district councils only have responsibility for certain operational aspects of traffic management, the burden of strategic transport planning falls upon the county councils in England and Wales and the Regional Councils in Scotland. Each of these local authorities has the duty of formulating its own local plans and policies, in consultation with the Regional Office of the Department of Transport.

While all county and regional councils operate as local planning authorities, the situation with respect to transport is rather more varied. Each council has to prepare overall policies relating to transport in the form of *Transport Policies and Programme* documents (Chapter 1). These rolling plans are the basis upon which local authority funding is identified and cover matters such as road improvement and maintenance schedules and operating subsidies for public transport (road and rail). In addition to this task, however, in the metropolitan areas there are also *passenger transport authorities* (PTAs), a concept first established under the 1968 Transport Act for five areas: South-east Lancashire/North-west Cheshire (SELNEC – now Greater Manchester), Merseyside, Tyneside, Greater Glasgow and the West Midlands. After 1972 local government re-organisation, South and West Yorkshire were added to the list and the Greater Glasgow PTA transferred to the Strathclyde Regional Council. It is the duty of the PTAs to provide a 'properly integrated and efficient system of public transport to meet the needs of the area', which they seek to discharge through a *Passenger Transport Executive* (PTE) made up of transport planners and other professional staff. The PTEs are responsible for the management and operation of all the former municipal passenger transport undertakings, for securing the provision of other public transport services in their areas by taking over or reaching operating agreements with private concerns, and under the 1980 Transport Act, for administering local rail services provided by British Rail. The metropolitan areas and the Strathclyde Regional Council therefore have an important executive function which goes beyond the powers customarily operating in town and country planning, and which notionally provides a significant tool which may be used to achieve wider land use planning objectives.

Non-metropolitan county councils also have passenger transport responsibilities in that they are to work to secure a 'co-ordinated and efficient system for their area', but they do not have a PTA or PTE and have no responsibility for operations. The same applies for the other Scottish regional and island authorities. In London, a newly formed London Transport Board was established in 1984, quite independent of the GLC, and

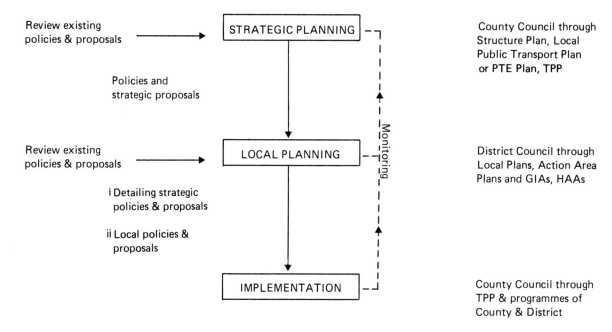

Source: A W McMillen (1978) The role of structure plans and local plans in transport planning,
Traffic Engineering and Control, June, pp294—5

Figure 6.2   The Transport Planning Process

to have responsibility for bus and tube services, although not for the BR network which is so important for commuter travel into the metropolis.

District councils have no responsibility for public transport planning, but 47 non-metropolitan districts have taken over the operation of those bus fleets formerly owned by the local municipality. Such a system may well be helpful in achieving local plan objectives, but all other bus services are provided by the National Bus Company through its 30 subsidiaries (48% of total vehicle mileage), or by the 5000 or so private operators (5% of total vehicle mileage).

Under the 1978 Transport Act, the non-metropolitan counties have to produce an annual *Public Transport Plan* (PTP) showing how the county intends to fulfill its public transport duties. The metropolitan counties had to produce such a plan when they were first established, but there was no requirement for them to be updated subsequently. Under the 1983 Transport Act, however, they are required to submit a three-year plan, annually, describing the level of transport services and facilities that will be provided and the general level and structure of fares that will be charged for these services.

At a strategic level TPPs and PTPs should be compatible with the statutory development plan (Fig 6.2), and in turn the Structure Plan will aim to reconcile transport requirements with the planned patterns of land uses, with local plans implementing detailed schemes. The county council, of course, remains the highway authority with responsibility for maintaining the fabric of the road system. Town planners are involved at both county and district level, with most non-metropolitan counties maintaining a Transportation Unit. Here, planners work on need assessment studies, problems of accessibility, the environmental impact of road schemes, traffic forecasts and predictions, public transport marketing schemes, the encouragement of voluntary transport schemes etc. In the metropolitan counties much of this technical work is undertaken by the PTE, but the county planning department still retains a transport section to deal with strategic issues. In both cases, working parties representing planners and operators meet frequently as an aid to policy making. In theory the potential exists to achieve the long awaited and widely acclaimed goal of transport planners, that of a fully integrated land use-transportation planning process. The extent to which this has been achieved is debatable and some of the practical difficulties are best illustrated with reference to the specific case of public transport planning.

Land Use Planning and Public Transport

While the influence of particular land use planning decisions may extend for several generations, the capacity of the local authority to plan and provide for the public transport implications of those decisions has proved much less effective. Since the 1968 Transport Act, both the PTEs and the non-metropolitan counties have sought to achieve balance and integration of the various transport services. Operations have been rationalised, standardised fare systems introduced, bus and rail services co-ordinated and new interchanges constructed, yet with few exceptions, patronage has continued to decline. The reasons for this contraction are varied and interconnected, but we can identify five principal causes.

i) Operating climate The spiral of decline in public transport patronage (reduction in passengers – increased fares – further reduction in patronage) was already well established by the late 1960's. While car owning was growing steadily, 20 years of land use planning had paradoxically created areas which were becoming increasingly more expensive to serve by public transport. Decentralisation and suburbanisation had resulted in lower population densities and a reduced level of demand for public transport on or around the routes radiating from town centres. While the planned separation of land uses had increased the necessity to travel, it was becoming more apparently expensive and inconvenient to do so other than by private car. While this may now be identified as a 'design fault', it is worth bearing in mind that the personal mobility afforded by the private car was seen as a rising and reasonable expectation for the majority of the population, and the disbenefits were not foreseen.

ii) Ability to integrate While the PTEs are 'owner operators', the same does not apply to the non metropolitan counties who are unable to exercise the same degree of control over the network. Some manage to achieve this in part by giving some level of support to all operators that qualify for revenue receipt, rather than concentrating on the most needy routes. In this way, they can begin to move some way towards comprehensive network support and planning, enabling the county to integrate transport planning with other strategic objectives, although it is really only planning by default. The counties can only implement policies by persuasion and

not compulsion so their role is primarily one of co-ordination in a partnership with operators and local communities. Despite these difficulties, the range of public transport options in rural areas has certainly increased. Innovations include the well-known post buses, public use of school buses, car sharing and social car schemes, community mini buses, shared taxis, transport for the disabled, tourist services and special fare strategies to meet local circumstances. Central government has encouraged the experimental development of such schemes by setting up *Rural Transport Experimental Areas* (RUTEX) in the mid-late 1970's and *Trial Areas* in 1980.

While the relevance of these rural strategies is being considered for urban areas, the task of co-ordination in the metropolitan areas is more difficult than might be apparent, partly for institutional reasons. In four of the six metropolitan counties, PTE's already existed before local government reform, and they had, therefore, developed their own forms of organisation and operation long before takeover in 1974. These have tended to persist and allowed the PTEs to maintain a measure of independence from their parent authority. Mention has already been made of the difficulties, too, in Greater London.

iii) Co-ordination and balance Government policy towards transport has for many years been based on the belief that it is possible to achieve co-ordination of the various transport services through natural competition in the market place. In reality, the competition between modes is very unequal, since roads and their users are permitted a highly privileged position. Unlike the rail network, there is no direct attribution of the cost of maintaining the road network to its users. Moreover, the tax levied on vehicles does not relate to the amount of use that each vehicle makes of the road system. The application of road pricing would reveal the true relative costs of public versus private use. This would encourage drivers to make a conscious assessment of the best way to travel and provide transport authorities with the means of pursuing a fully balanced strategy.

iv) Revenue and financial support Since the 1968 Transport Act formally recognised the subsidisation of public transport operations, arguments have raged over the extent to which provision should be based on economic or social considerations. The issue came to a head in the early 1980's with a series of court cases brought by ratepayers against a number of transport authorities over the legality of their level of subsidy of uneconomic operations for social reasons. It appeared that under the 1969 London Act, the passenger transport authority had a responsibility to break even, whereas the 1968 Transport Act, which covered the six provincial passenger transport authorities makes no such stipulation. This effectively meant that while it was illegal to subsidise fares in London, it was perfectly proper elsewhere if it enabled authorities to discharge their responsibilities in law.

Relative to other West European countries, revenue support for public transport in Britain is low, and this is often advanced as a major reason for its decline. Comparisons are difficult, however, and raw operating statistics do not always take into account the relative level of government support, different types of planning system and socio-economic contrasts between countries.

v) Transport planning methodology During the 1960's and early 1970's, transport planning tended to concentrate on the supply of transport infrastructure to accommodate increasing levels of traffic. Travellers were seen in aggregate terms, and transport problems were usually defined as engineering problems which required technical solutions. Surprisingly for an industry with so much customer contact, little or no attention was paid to consumer demand as networks and service standards were barely modified while population distribution and urban environments underwent rapid change. That such a situation should develop partly reflects the engineering background of many transport planners at the time, and the urge for a 'scientific' approach, but also reflects the compartmentalism of local authority operations before the introduction of more 'corporate' approaches after the 1972 reform. A more 'responsive' style of local government, new enthusiasm for 'client-based' approaches to planning, and a government commitment to the market economy have combined to change approaches to transport planning towards a more active engagement with the potential market. The widely adopted off-peak fare policy is one example of this move away from standardised operation. It is likely that operators will be encouraged further in this direction by the 1983 Transport Act which requires PTEs to justify their level of transport services and the fares they charge in terms of level of demand and user benefits.

6.4   CONCLUSION

This chapter has tended to dwell upon one strand of transport, that of public transport, and ignore other areas where planners also play an important role. Even if different emphasis had been selected, however, the conclusions would have been similar. Central government direction and guidance in transport policy has often been vague, inconsistent and at times contradictory. The benefits of working toward the balanced and co-ordinated provision of transport facilities at a national level can be seen from the experiences of other W European countries. In Britain, transport policy has been truly incremental and affords yet another example of where issues can become clouded by political polarisation. In such an uncompromising climate, transport planners do well to achieve what they do.

Further reading

For a wide ranging introduction to transport and a useful reference manual see D Maltby & H P White 1982 *Transport in the United Kingdom* (MacMillan)
Two volumes of edited conference papers offer valuable insights into the relationship between land use and transportation planning – R W Cresswell (ed) 1979 *Urban Planning and Public Transport* and A P Young & R W Cresswell 1982 *The Urban Transport Future*, both published by Construction Press.
The political context is well illustrated by D H McKay & A W Cox 1979 *The Politics of Urban Change* (Croom Helm), while a refreshingly different market oriented perspective is provided by J Hibbs 1982 Transport without Politics? *Hobart Paper 95*.
On relative levels of mobility experienced see M Hillman et al 1976 *Transport Realities and Planning Policy* (PEP)
P D Banister & P Hall (eds) 1981 *Transport and Public Policy Planning* (Mansell) is particularly good on methodological developments.
As case studies, and also as valuable sources of information on methods, legislation and operations it is worth consulting individual PTPs.

CHAPTER 7
RETAILING

Although some planners see retailing as merely concerned with the location of shopping premises, it has a much wider sweep as part of the total marketing and distribution function, and has undergone dramatic change since the early 1960's. While it is extremely difficult to identify cause and effect, retail change has resulted from the interplay of three main groups of factors which are outlined in Fig 7.1 and include changes in consumer behaviour, retail organisation and the retailing environment.

able incomes affected retailing. So did the spatial trends of suburbanisation and decentralisation. Incomes are higher and a higher proportion is spent on retail goods, aided by the increasing availability of credit. More specifically, *spending patterns* have altered in favour of comparison goods and services as opposed to convenience goods. Advances in domestic technology and increased use of kitchen hardware have reduced the amount of time taken up by domestic chores. Much of the time released in this way has been absorbed by increases in employment for married women. Both trends have reduced the time spent in regular shopping.

7.1   TRENDS IN RETAILING

Changes in Consumer Behaviour

Most of the changes in lifestyle referred to earlier, including increased levels of mobility and larger dispos-

Changes in Retail Organisation

The period since 1960 has been one of rationalisation and innovation in retail organisation. The market share

Figure 7.1   Elements of retail change in Britain 1950–1985

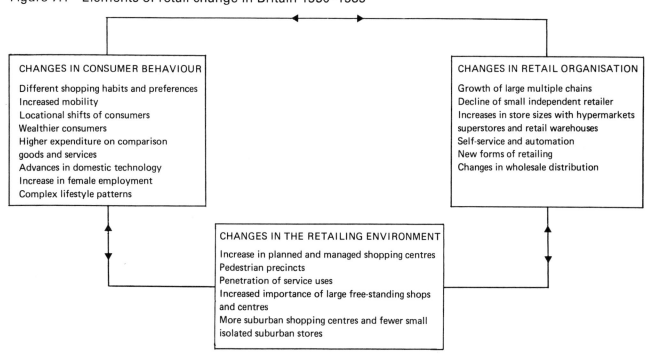

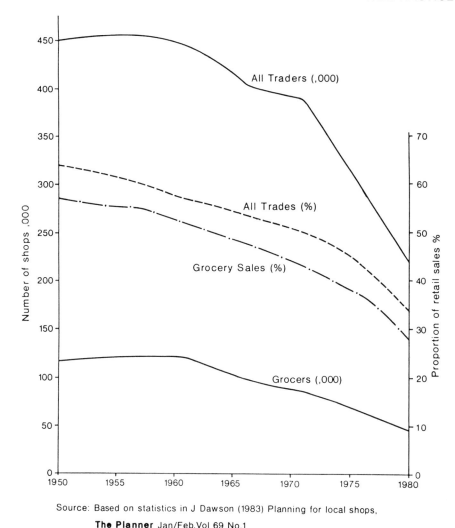

Source: Based on statistics in J Dawson (1983) Planning for local shops,
The Planner Jan/Feb.Vol 69 No.1

Figure 7.2   Estimates of fixed shop numbers and market share of independent retailers (including those
             in contractual chains)

of the large multiple chain has grown, and as can be seen in Fig 7.2 that of the small independent retailer has declined, although the two are not always causally related. We now have a situation where 25% of the total national retail market is in the hands of only 10 companies. In food retailing, 64% of Britain's packaged grocery market is in the hands of only 7 companies.

Accompanying this process, store size has increased very significantly, in association with the growth of self service and automation as well as the emergence of several new forms of retail structure such as franchising and discounting. Possibly the most significant development has been the development of the hypermarket and superstore. In a relatively short time they have achieved

a position of pre-eminence in food and general household retailing. This is mainly because of their ability to offer a wide range of goods at competitively low prices, together with a high degree of convenience, particularly for the car owner. The same set of advantages also applies to discount retail warehouses selling furniture and carpets, DIY and electrical goods. These have also moved out of, or have rejected, traditional locations in favour of sites which enable them to realise economies of scale, to discount prices and achieve high volume turnover. Together with hypermarkets and superstores they have generated controversy in planning circles as this new form of retailing has spread throughout the country (Fig 7.3).

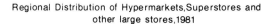

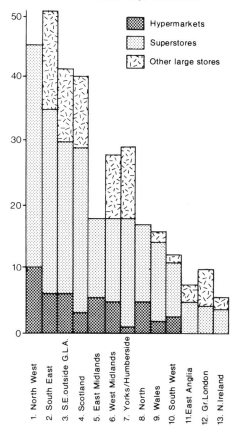

Source: P.Jones (1982) Hypermarkets and superstores: future growth or saturation? **Estates Gazette** May 29th Vol 262

Figure 7.3 Hypermarkets and superstores

Changes in the Retailing Environment

Since 1945 the retailing environment has undergone a quite dramatic change in *appearance*. In the late 1940's and early 1950's, priority was give to the re-building of war-damaged centres and it was at this time that the modern pedestrian precinct first appeared as 'New Town' practices were applied to cities such as Coventry and Plymouth. During the 'fifties and 'sixties shopping (re)development was a boom industry which affected all major British towns. As the momentum was continued into the 'seventies many cities were provided with completely new or rebuilt shopping centres, developed in many cases by partnerships of property companies and local authorities. Some indication of the scale of change is given by Fig 7.4. It can be seen that over this time span there has been a move away from quite small open air schemes to a much bigger, enclosed type of development.

In order to participate profitably in the processes of higher consumer spending, banks, building societies, finance and insurance houses have appeared in ever-growing numbers in shopping centres. Equally, increased numbers of travel agents, estate agents, cafes and restaurants are also clamouring for locations on or near major shopping streets in order to benefit from greater expenditure on service goods.

The retailing environment created over the past 35 years is one of immense variety. Much of the new development has taken place in traditional shopping centres, but there has also been a growth of retailing in non-central locations. The old traditional hierarchy of shopping centres has now been distorted by the influence of many new types of shopping facility supplementing new and redeveloped town centre schemes with large shopping districts, hypermarket centres (based around anchor traders), multi-purpose centres (retail, commercial, recreational and residential), and speciality centres (craftware, antiques and leisure outlets).

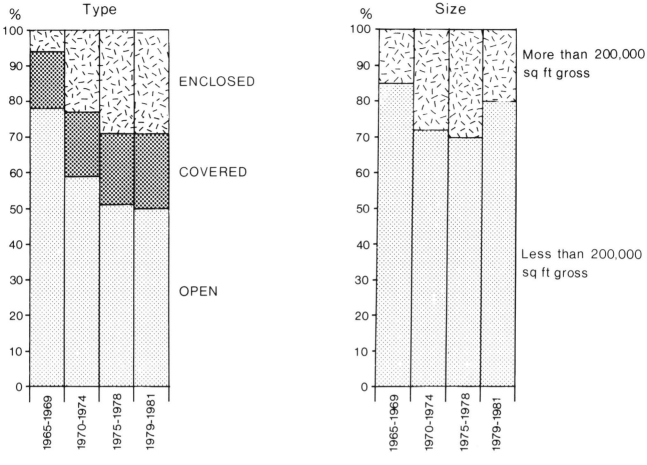

NOTE   Shopping schemes defined as a comprehensive retail development of at least
         50,000 sq ft gross lettable area

Source: Hillier Parker Research- **British Shopping Developments** 1978,1979,1980,1981

Figure 7.4   New shopping schemes 1965–81

7.2 LOCAL PLANNING AND RETAILING

Even though it has proved difficult to secure stated objectives, housing, transport, employment and the environment are at least recognised policy areas for both central and local government, which may be more than is the case of retailing. Local authorities, it is true, have long maintained an interest in retail planning, but central government has played a very minor role, and the number of DOE circulars on retailing, for instance, is somewhat fewer than in other policy areas. In some respects this is surprising, since retail activity is profoundly affected by government economic policies and, indeed, is one of the major instruments of those poli-

cies, as well as being a barometer of economic well-being. Yet as the very epitome of the market economy, the planning of retailing is almost a contradiction in terms.

Retailing and the Development Plan

The basic role of the retail planner is to reconcile the various demands of developers, retailers and consumers, whilst at the same time considering the broader relationships between retailing and such factors as transport, housing, employment and questions of amenity. We can see retail planning operating, then, at both structure and local plan levels.

A   RETAIL PLANNING POLICIES IN STRUCTURE PLANS

Policy Area	Number of Structure Plans		
	with policies	without policies	no response/ not applic.
Control or encouragement of hypermarkets and superstores	55	3	
Local shop provision	46	12	
Mobile shops	5	51	2
Retailing from industrial areas	44	14	
Quasi-retail activity in retail districts e.g. Building Socs. etc.	7	51	
Control or encouragement of large comparison goods stores	36	22	
Inner city regeneration through retail investment	25	20	13
Maintenance of an existing retail hierarchy	50	7	1
Expansion of retail floorspace for certain levels of hierarchy	30	25	3
Servicing of shops in established shopping districts	15	43	
Provision of car parking for consumers	29	29	
Shopping centres in refurbished historical buildings	5	53	

B   STRUCTURE PLAN POLICIES AFFECTING RETAIL DEVELOPMENT IN RURAL AREAS OF S.W. ENGLAND

	Number of retailing Policies	Policies influencing rural activities			
		Encourage Village Shops	Concentrate New Dev'ts in Main Centres	Limit out of town retailing	Existence of key sett't policies
AVON	5		*	*	*
CORNWALL	No direct policy statements on retailing				
DEVON	8	*		*	*
S E DORSET	5		*	*	not applic.
DORSET (rest)	Not yet available				
GLOUCESTER	7	*		*	*
SOMERSET	5			*	*
N E WILTSHIRE	5	*		*	*
S WILTSHIRE	4		*	*	*
W WILTSHIRE	3		*	*	*

Sources: A   S Burt, J A Dawson & L Sparks (1983) Structure plans and retailing policies, **The Planner** 69 11–12

B   G Shaw (1982) Structure plan policies in rural areas a case study of South West England, **Service Industries Review,** 2 38–51

Table 17   Retailing Issues in Structure Plans

i) Structure plan policies aim to deal with those aspects of retailing deemed to be of strategic importance to a county. A survey of structure plans carried out in 1982 revealed twelve such policy areas relating to various aspects of structural change (see Table 17). The general picture that emerged was that few counties had a comprehensive package of retail planning policies, most being content to address themselves to specific issues, usually in a reactive fashion. Broadly speaking the majority of policies sought to maintain the status quo of the existing shopping heirarchy, despite the great changes which we have noted already. Certainly a great many forecasts of strategic shopping floorspace requirements are made on this basis even though there has been substantial criticism of their validity, and the demand for 'floorspace' of itself is not sufficiently strategic, given the varied character of retail trading.

ii) Local plan policies are by nature much more specific. Although shopping is probably one of the few topics suited to comprehensive treatment in a subject plan, most local plans for retailing take the form of district plans, or where these do not yet exist, are in the form of policy statements or guidelines. Once again, the starting point of most local retail planning policies is usually an assessment of floorspace totals for the area to be covered by the plan. This is then disaggregated in terms of type and location. In addition, local plans have usually addressed themselves to matters associated with car parking, pedestrianisation and sites for future retail developments. A set of district shopping policies can be seen in Table 18 where it seems that in terms of scope and definition, there is general conformity with the issues listed under structure plan policies in Table 17, although it must be said that county-district disputes over specific allocations and the interpretation of policy are quite common.

Retail Planning Issues

The notion of an heirarchical arrangement of service centres still seems to dominate most retail planning issues. For many years, urban geographers and planners alike have been persuaded by the concepts of central place theory which first appeared in 1933. On the basis of the sizes of *trade areas* and the *centrality* values of places, it is possible to develop nested *hierarchies* of shopping centres at both the inter and intra urban scales. This conceptual framework has been used as a basis for developing sophisticated models of shopping behaviour given certain allocations of floorspace, especially in the 1960's and the early 1970's. Currently there is very little research activity of this type, largely due to the heavy demands that are made in manpower and financial terms. Nevertheless, the basic premises persist, and in consequence most retail planning issues revolve around the insistence of planners that the existing heirarchy of shopping centres must be maintained. The existence of this common theme can be illustrated by two particularly contentious issues.

i) Hypermarkets, superstores and warehouses are often opposed on the grounds that business will be diverted from existing smaller shops, thereby threatening the viability of established centres and intensifying the deprivation already felt by the poor and immobile. Even in most Enterprise Zones, where the accent is on freedom from planning restraint, maximum size limits on retail developments 'in the interests of existing shops' effectively excludes large stores from such locations. When challenged by appeal, the local planning authority usually finds it difficult to justify these assertions. The DOE makes the task difficult from the start by advising that it is not the role of the planning authority to attempt to stem competition within the retail trade or to protect commercial interests. In the event, such studies that have been done of the impact of hypermarkets/superstores seems to suggest that any competition that is created is between like stores, rather than with existing centres, and in fact far greater diversion of custom seems to occur when stores are built not in peripheral locations or in the suburbs but in existing centres 'to strengthen the existing hierarchy'. Experience has now shown that the out of town store, with its customary emphasis upon food and household goods, is unlikely to affect the performance of town centres, since central shopping areas remain the most attractive location for comparison shopping. Equally, it has also been found that because such large stores attract customers from wide areas, their impact upon particular small outlets is diffused, although it does, of course, remain. On the question of restricting the shopping choice of the poor and immobile, the nature and extent of impact is not clear. In some cases, their needs are met by those developers who prefer to locate their new stores in inner city and suburban locations, in preference to sites on the urban fringe. In others, special bus services are often provided which offer the shopper the added convenience of shop door transport. There is also an argument that a more widespread distribution of shops will offer a far higher level of convenience and accessibility than that afforded by the conventionalised hierarchy, although admittedly it may become more difficult to reach a particular type of store under such circumstances.

THE RETAIL, WHOLESALE AND SERVICE TRADES

SHOPPING AND SERVICES

7.56   It is intended that encouragement should be given to the maintenance of prosperous and varied local shops and services. At a time when the costs of travel by both private and public transport are increasing, it is considered important that a wide range of food and normal household goods should be obtainable locally. However, it must be recognised that as a small town in a rural area Lewes cannot provide the volume of trade required to support the range and type of such shopping available in larger centres. The proximity of Brighton as an inhibiting influence on the growth of shopping in Lewes, especially for clothing and furnishings, is explained in 4.79. Nevertheless, it is suggested that the developing specialist shop and service sector in Lewes is likely to attract custom from a wide area on the strength of the goods or services available, and that this sector is both supported by and an attraction to visitors.

7.57   Small, old shops and off-centre locations normally pose no problems to the latter type of business, and indeed may be an advantage. However, whilst recognising the value of neighbourhood shops, it is considered that the existing diffuse shopping area is a disadvantage as far as shopping for day-to-day needs is concerned and that it may serve as a deterrent to shoppers. It is proposed, therefore, to encourage the establishment of a definite shopping focus in the Cliffe/Eastgate area, mainly for this type of shopping.

7.58   There have been several changes of use recently of shops to building societies and similar office uses in the upper High Street. This has resulted in a loss of shopping facilities and has had a blighting effect on the shopping frontages. It is proposed that the established shopping area in the upper part of High Street between the castle and the war memorial should not be allowed to change entirely into office or other uses. The reason is not only because of the loss of facilities for residents and workers in the area, but also because the High Street would lose vitality and interest for visitors to the town's major tourist area. Inevitably the existing mix of shops will change as some firms move to the Cliffe. Over a period of time, therefore, a greater propor — tion of specialist and quality shops and cafes could develop which would retain the attraction and vitality of the area.

7.59   The function of Lewes as a shopping centre both for day-to day needs and for specialist goods will be encouraged.

7.60   In the High Street and Cliffe High Street, between Eastgate Street and South Street, there will be a presumption in favour of retaining the ground floors of properties in retail use.

7.61   A shopping focus will be retained in the High Street — on the north side between Castle Gate and Fisher Street, on the south side between Walwers Lane and St. Martins Lane — in order to retain a shopping/service element for residents and visitors to this part of the town.

Reasons:

7.62   To achieve aim 6.4 (prosperity of shops and services).

Implementation:

7.63   (a)   Through development control.

(b)   Schemes for traffic management, public transport and car parking in these areas will be prepared with policy 7.59 as a priority (see special area policies and proposals for the Historic Core, the Cliffe and transport proposals).

(c)   Elsewhere in the town changes to or from retail/service trade uses will be dealt with under the appropriate general development policy.

RETAIL WAREHOUSES

7.64   There are no retail warehouses in Lewes at present. This is a growing and sometimes controversial form of trading and it is considered that a policy should be formulated in the Local Plan. It is considered that in view of the new shopping developments the trading position in the town should be allowed to consolidate before any such operations are allowed. Furthermore, in view of the shortage of industrial land, it is not considered that these activities should be allowed to further reduce the supply. However, ancillary sales from genuine warehouses, such as those of builders merchants, are acceptable.

7.65   Retail warehouses will not be permitted in Lewes. Retail sales which are purely ancillary to a wholesale operation will be acceptable.

Reasons:

7.66   To safeguard the prosperity of town centre shops — aim 6.4.

THE MARKETS

7.68   The present market occupies a confined site on the edge of the Historic Core and experiences access and parking difficulties. It is conceivable that at some time in the future it may wish to expand and/or relocate onto a larger site in order to overcome these problems.

7.69   The expansion and/or relocation of the existing agricultural and retail markets will be supported in principle.

Reasons:

7.70   Lewes is a traditional market town and it is considered that the agricultural and retail markets are not only a service to the community of the area, but are a part of the character of the town.

Implementation:

7.71   (a)   Through development control, subject to acceptability under general development policies.

(b)   Through powers of the local authorities as landowners/highway authority where appropriate.

(c)   See also Section G: Malling Brooks.

Source: Town of Lewes District Plan
                Written Statement July 1979

Table 18   Retailing and the Local Plan; Lewes, Sussex

ii) The growth of service uses in shopping centres Many local planning authorities have a presumption against uses such as building societies, banks, estate agents, insurance offices, betting shops and finance houses in prime shopping areas. It is argued that if allowed to continue unabated, the growth of such uses and the subsequent loss of shopping floor space will affect the viability of the shopping centre. Many authorities have therefore formulated policies which aim to restrict the incidence of such use. Examination of these policies, however, revealed that the vast majority were not based on any hard evidence of the repercussions, but were largely intuitive. What little research that has been carried out on the pattern reveals, in reality, that the loss of retail floorspace is much less than is generally believed. Moreover, surveys of consumer behaviour have revealed that most of the 'quasi-retail' uses provide services of a form that contribute more to the retail viability of a centre than do such uses as TV rental shops and gas/electricity showrooms which are a commonly accepted feature of shopping centres. On the other hand, these 'quasi-retail' outlets acknowledge the problem, having a vested interest themselves in maintaining a balance of service and retail uses and the viability of the shopping centre that attracted them in the first place.

These two examples have served to illustrate the way in which conventional views of the shopping heirarchy are being challenged by the 'natural' evolution of the retail trades. At the other end of the scale, however, there is evidence to suggest that benefits *are* to be gained, particularly in rural areas, by the planned maintenance of the small retail outlet, the lowest tier of the shopping heirarchy. Practice in several European countries has now been emulated in Britain by the application of government assistance, through CoSIRA, to the management of the country store. The closure of such outlets has been a significant manifestation of opportunity deprivation in rural areas, and raises a fundamental planning issue in the balance between social and economic utility.

7.3   CONCLUSION

Retail planning policies have probably been applied more rigorously in Britain than in any other developed country, and have variously retarded, assisted and accelerated different aspects of retail change. Yet retail planning as a specialism has not received the same investment in research and staffing than many other policy areas and seems relatively ill-equipped to deal with the planning environment of the 1980's.

Relations between planners and retailers are poor, with the latter claiming that it has yet to be decided whether retailing should be seen as an economic or social activity. It is felt that planners are unnecessarily cautious and conservative in their response to retailing innovations, and that this is due to their limited understanding of the retail function. They also claim that the retailer is better equipped to make policy decisions than the planners since their investment in research and surveys of retail potential is usually much greater than that of the local planning authority. Many retailers are of the opinion that retail planning policies in Britain have served to perpetuate inefficient patterns of retail location, ultimately to the cost of the consumer in terms of price, convenience and choice. Given the increasing cost of public transport, for example, a case can be made for an expansion of more local shopping facilities and a much more restricted or specialised role for town centres.

These are the sort of issues that retail planning will have to address if it is to achieve its primary objective of maximising benefits to the community whilst reducing the incidence of negative effects which might result from new retail development. In order to do this effectively, detailed investigations of the various impacts are required for different types of retailing and for different groups of consumers. Only then will the local planning authority be in a position to make informed decisions on retail planning applications and formulate effective retail planning policies.

Further reading

For good general introductions to retail change in Britain see P M Jones 1979 Retail planning: recent trends 1, 2 & 3, *Estates Gazette*, June 9, 16 and 23, and J A Bamfield 1980, The changing face of British retailing, *Nat West Bank Review*, May. For a more detailed investigation of many of the points raised in this chapter see C M Guy 1980 *Retail Location and Retail Planning in Britain* (Saxon House). A useful introduction to various aspects of retail geography can be found in J A Dawson (ed) 1980 *Retail Geography* (Croom Helm). A valuable source of comparative material on retail planning trends and procedures in various EEC countries is R L Davies (ed) 1979 *Retail Planning in the European Community* (Saxon House).

CHAPTER 8
THE ENVIRONMENT

8.1 AMENITY AND THE ENVIRONMENT

Although all land use planning is concerned with the environment, certain aspects are conventionally assigned a more specific 'environmental' label. Some activities, such as the control of advertising, may be regarded as cosmetic rather than fundamental, but others, such as the designation of greenbelt or cherished landscape may be of a strategic nature and form a major framework for planning. Most of the policies considered below relate to concepts of amenity, yet they are also sometimes a matter of good husbandry and owe more to concerns for longer term resource conservation than more immediate social well-being. Thus modern environmentalists would oppose the sterilisation of mineral resources and urban expansion on high quality agricultural land, but such ideas were espoused in the inter-war years and indeed stimulated the first Land Utilisation Survey in 1936. It was certainly hoped that the powers given to local planning authorities in 1947 would ensure the implementation of such policies, but in the event more land was transferred from agricultural to urban use in the thirty years after the Act than in the thirty years before, much of it for residential use. Thus in a provocative article in 1977, Alice Coleman showed how housing development around the Thames estuary, including Basildon New Town and Thamesmead, had taken up 18.5km^2 of open land. Unfortunately this had been almost entirely offset by a loss of 18km^2 of housing through clearance schemes within the former built-up areas. Such a result was by no means in the minds of those who saw planning as the obvious way to secure high standards of amenity while maintaining an efficient use of land.

The concept of amenity is very hard to define and is not static. In a sanitary sense the provision of the 'basic amenities' has long been used as an indicator of residential well-being. The concept is far wider, however, and less easy to identify in such a precise way, for it may relate to the presence of desirable facilities (or the absence of undesirable activities), a particular style of architecture or form of landscape, or it may relate to less tangible criteria of ambience or social status. In short, amenity is largely a matter of taste and it is all too easy for standards of amenity to be determined by the taste of the planners. In many instances, amenity seems definable only when it is threatened by some change, and it often seems that it is only when an aspect of amenity has been lost in one place that we can recognise it being threatened in another. Thus the massive changes which overtook many city centres in the 1960's highlighted the need for care in others, while the destruction of 'traditional' farming landscapes either by urban encroachment or modern agricultural methods has similarly encouraged a cherishing of less-changed areas. The antidote to loss of amenity, therefore, has often been seen as the inhibiting of change, *preservation*, or the management of its impact, *conservation*.

A considerable amount of activity in this field requires the confirmation or approval of the Secretary of State for the Environment, and indeed only the Secretary of State (advised by the Countryside Commission) can designate cherished landscapes. Nevertheless, because of the fine grain at which much environmental planning has to operate, the major burden falls upon the local planning authority. Most of the issues relating to the natural environment – greenbelt, landscape appraisal and the extraction of minerals – are matters of structure planning and so are handled at county level. In contrast, matters of the built environment are more often the concern of the district planning authority.

8.2 PLANNING IN THE NATURAL ENVIRONMENT

Because so much planning activity is directed towards settlements, it is easy to overlook the *country* element in our town and country planning system. The need to conserve the countryside, however, was a significant aspiration of the founders of the town and country planning movement at the beginning of the present century. Similarly, the persistent expansion of urban areas, and the lengthening tentacles of ribbon development motivated many of the proponents of post-war planning legislation who were also equally moved by the desirability of enhancing public access to the countryside.

Besides being an important national resource in terms of agricultural production, the countryside has also been seen as a repository of recuperative and recreational qualities, a rural idyll which grew out of the Romantic Movement of a century and a half ago. Two guiding concepts have thus underpinned much of rural planning: the protection of the countryside from urban expansion and its promotion as a place for recreation. The practice of agriculture itself, however, has never been viewed as a matter for land use planning legislation and under the 1947 Act, agriculture and forestry were not regarded as 'development'. In consequence, the principal land uses in the countryside and which, moreover, have the greatest impact upon its appearance are outside planning law except insofar as they require the provision of dwelling houses. Planning has thus played a minor role as agriculture has been transformed by a combination of technical innovation, EEC/government pricing policies and massive new investment in land. Because these changes have had important consequences for the visual amenity of the countryside, the richness of its natural flora and fauna and the quality and variety of its vernacular architecture, there has been growing concern from the planning profession, the Countryside Commission and conservation interests that agriculture should not continue to operate without reference to amenity considerations, and that at the least, planning control should be extended to all constructions associated with farming and forestry.

This debate has become most pointed in areas of special landscape quality and at sites of special scientific interest (see below), but it is not the only point of conflict in the countryside: mineral working, water gathering and forestry have all been seen as competing with agriculture, and especially in upland areas, as detrimental to public amenity. There are, of course, attendant social problems which have planning consequences as agricultural populations have been reduced, especially in the remoter areas, and as the countryside has come under increasing pressure to accommodate those from urban areas who wish either to visit or to live in attractive rural surroundings.

Greenbelt

Perhaps the most well known of all planning concepts, the idea of an identified stretch of countryside acting as a *cordon sanitaire* to protect the countryside from unlimited urban expansion was first put into practice around London subsequent to Abercrombie's Greater London Plan (1944). Under the 1947 Town and Country Planning Act the principle was formally established in the county maps of the surrounding Home Counties. Under Circular 42/55 similar zones were proposed around all the conurbations, around the rapidly expanding towns of S. Hampshire, and around historic centres such as Oxford, Cambridge and York. In the event, these proposals acted only as informal guides, and even the statutory London Green Belt suffered from considerable development pressure over the 1960's and 1970's. Nevertheless, despite the fact that greenbelt policies have been difficult to implement, they have been taken up as a major tool of structure planning, affirmed under Circular 22/80 as a vital means of preventing urban sprawl. Figure 8.1 shows the concept applied to Huddersfield, where it can be clearly seen as a belt almost encircling the town. Its outer limits, however, conform to the boundaries of the former county borough (and in turn to medieval townships) rather than to obviously identifiable landscape units.

The familiar arguments against green belts were rehearsed most recently in 1982–3. With some justification, the House Builders' Federation pointed out that within designated greenbelt there were often significant areas of derelict land or open space which fulfilled no useful purpose. Around London, alone, it was claimed that there were 22 large sites, sufficient for 4,000 new houses. There have also been suggestions that the NHS, which owns over 20,000 ha of green belt land, should be allowed to release for development those sites which it no longer requires for institutional use, since the mere provision of open space rather than open access is of no particular benefit. Under Conservative administrations the DOE is susceptible to such arguments and its position in 1983 was that greenbelts were themselves most effective as long as sufficient land was allocated for development within their confines. So authorities were encouraged not to draw the inner edge of belts too close to the built up area, nor to include merely small pockets or green wedges which were hardly the extensive zones of unbuilt-up land originally intended. It could be argued, of course, that such small areas may be in some circumstances the most vital to maintain, and the issue principally rests upon the purpose of a green belt.

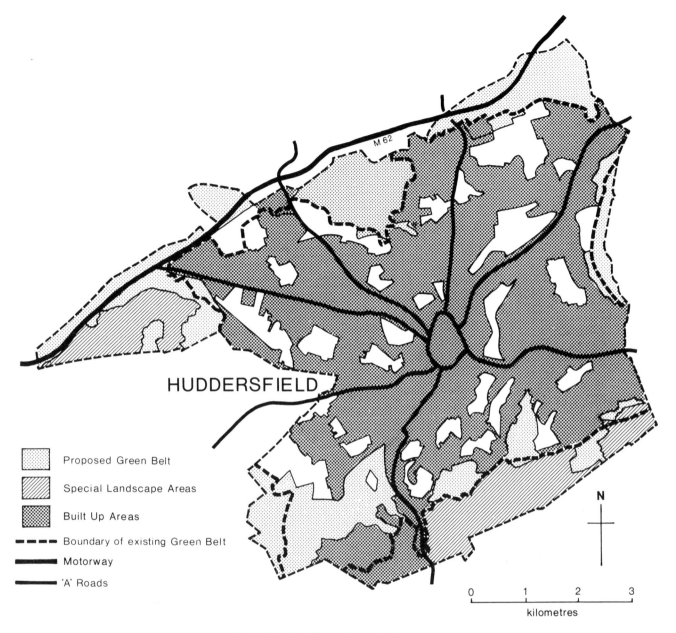

Figure 8.1   Kirklees M C   Huddersfield District Plan: Greenbelt

The belts proposed for Oxford, Cambridge and York were to help preserve the special character of those ancient cities. The Greater Manchester Structure Plan, which included perhaps the most comprehensive review of greenbelt policy ever undertaken, reaffirmed the policy as a means of deflecting and controlling urban expansion, even in the face of strong development pressure. In South Yorkshire on the other hand, the green belt was designated mainly to provide open country and the possibility for outdoor recreation within easy reach of people's homes. To these three criteria, Circular 14/84 added 'assisting in urban regener-ation', but whatever the case, it is still largely a matter of planning for urban areas, rather than positive planning of the countryside. There is merit in the argument that such policies inflate property values within green belts which may lead to un-looked for social changes, while stultifying development around the urban fringe on land which may not necessarily be put to productive agricultural use. Nevertheless, greenbelts have proved a useful planning tool. To be meaningful they clearly have to have a long life, however, a feature which was questioned during the preparation of Circular 14/84. Although the circular disappointed some in this regard, it does at least commit the greenbelts to being maintained, and it seems hard to conceive of them as being under general threat.

Cherished Landscapes

The preservation of special landscapes dedicated to public use and enjoyment was promoted as long ago as 1865 by the *Commons, Footpaths and Open Space Society* and since 1895 by the *National Trust*, but it was only with the National Parks and Access to the Countryside Act, 1949, that rural conservation was publicly espoused. Under the Act a National Parks Commission was created to designate extensive areas suitable for informal recreation as *National Parks* and smaller areas as *Areas of Outstanding Natural Beauty*, both to be confirmed by the responsible Minister. The ten national parks in England and Wales were designated by 1955, mainly in upland areas, and by 1968 25 AONBs had also been designated, mainly in lowland areas. The Act also enabled long distance footpaths to be designated, of which the first was the Pennine Way, and provided for the recording, creation and repair of rights of way, along with the designation of open 'access land'. The National Parks Commission's tasks related principally to the enjoyment of the countryside by walkers, ramblers and cyclists. As more people, many of them motorists, sought the pleasures of the countryside, however, the 1968 Countryside Act reconstituted the National Parks Commission as the Countryside Commission. To the National Parks Commission's initial tasks (a further 12 AONBs have been designated along with other long distance paths) was added a wider-ranging role in countryside matters. The Countryside Commission was re-formed in 1981 as a grant-in-aid body. It has only a modest budget, but as an officially sponsored 'ginger group' it advises government as well as private interests on matters of countryside enjoyment. Much of its effort is directed towards conservation, aiming to encourage the visitor and the rural resident on the careful use of the countryside in a variety of ways, from encouraging small schemes of countryside interpretation to wide-ranging and complex management agreements.

i) **National Parks** With the exception of the Lake District and the Peak District, which have specially constituted Planning Boards to act as the local planning authority, planning in the National Parks is reserved to the county councils who must establish a *National Park Committee* to have oversight of all functions except the preparation of development plans. The committees will be made up of a number of elected members from the county councils involved, and other members representing lay, local and conservation interests nominated by the Secretary of State. One of the special responsibilities of a national park committee is the production of a *National Park Plan* which is essentially an action-oriented plan which attempts to co-ordinate public and private land management in accordance with the objectives of the park. As such they are the fruit of extensive consultation and agreement with land holders and other interested parties, but they are not statutory plans and only require submission to the Countryside Commission and to the various district councils for comment at a draft stage. Table 19 illustrates the sort of issues dealt with in such a plan and an example of policy development to deal with the impact of visitor pressure with careful management of the rural heritage as the key issue. Procedures are otherwise the same inside the national parks as outside, save that the minor household and industrial developments permitted under the GDO regulations, 1981, are still subject to control, and the local planning authority may compulsorily acquire land for certain amenity purposes and can obtain grant aid for the preservation and enhancement of the natural beauty of the area.

National park planning authorities undoubtedly pay a great deal of attention to the maintenance of a high standard of amenity, but this will not necessarily be the deciding factor in determining the outcome of planning applications. Moreover, in so far as agriculture itself is beyond the scope of town and country planning legislation, and the general thrust of EEC and MAFF policies is towards agricultural methods which enhance productivity, often at the cost of the traditional appearance of the landscape, the conservation interest is very vulnerable. It would be fair to say that conservationist aspirations and practical policy making are often some distance apart in such circumstances, hence the importance of the national park plans. At the lowest level, therefore, National Park and AONB designation is little more than a signal to interpret planning legislation with a particular eye for amenity and as such conflict is inevitable.

ii) **Landscape evaluation** Attention to landscape quality extends beyond National Parks, AONBs and designated *Heritage Coasts* (after the 1970 Countryside Commission report 'The Coastal Heritage'), for the preparation of structure plans has involved extensive assessment of landscape quality. Although the techniques used have varied, the intention has been to identify those stretches of countryside which have *great*

The following issues were identified in the plan, for most of which policies were developed as in the example in (B) below:

A. ISSUES

LOSS TO NATURAL HERITAGE
Loss of broadleaved tree cover
Spread of conifers
Loss of wildlife and features of scientific interest

LOSS TO HISTORIC HERITAGE
Loss of remains and damage to sites of archaelogical interest
Dereliction of field barns
Disrepair of dry stone walls
Loss of existing architectural and historic interest
Alterations to road character

IMPACT OF NEW DEVELOPMENT
Visual impact of new buildings
Impact of modern farm buildings
Intrusiveness of public utilities
Impact of large scale mineral extraction
Reduction of public transport services

IMPACT OF VISITOR PRESSURE
Accumulation of litter and indiscriminate dumping of rubbish
Adverse environmental impact of road traffic
Provision of access
Management of rights of way
Environmental impact of the recreational use of caravans and tents
Demand for other visitor facilities
Heavy recreational use of popular sites
Problems relating to understanding and behaviour

B. EXAMPLE OF POLICY DEVELOPMENT

PROBLEMS RELATING TO UNDERSTANDING AND BEHAVIOUR

Not all present day visitors to the National Park are country-minded or behave sensibly and responsibly. Despite the efforts of the National Park Committee and various other organisations to remedy inconsiderate behaviour by attempting to raise the level of understanding of and respect for the countryside, the problem persists.

Policies

(i) Urge the Countryside Commission to enlist the support of the media in giving added national publicity to correct misconceptions concerning land ownership and rights of the public in national parks and in emphasising the special problems created for agriculture in the uplands by irresponsible and inconsiderate behaviour.

(ii) Further increase warden coverage.

(iii) Investigate the possible extension of information and interpretative services by the provision of small-scale low cost facilities in villages frequented by visitors.

(iv) Extend the range of its publications and the number of outlets for distribution within the National Park.

(v) Develop the use of Whernside Manor Cave and Fell Centre as a residential and day centre where the general public may, by participation and first hand experience, gain a greater appreciation of the countryside and, in particular, of the significance of its caves and associated landforms.

(vi) Liaise with local education authorities and schools regarding the use of the National Park for environmental studies and outdoor pursuits.

(vii) Encourage the development of a programme of farm open days at peak visitor periods and the establishment of farm trails.

(viii) Continue to support existing voluntary rescue services.

(ix) Provide limited sponsorship to approved university research projects and engage, or enlist the voluntary provision of, specialist assistance on specific surveys and other studies designed to increase knowledge of particular aspects of the Dales relevant to the statutory responsibilities of the National Park Committee.

(x) Develop a bibliography of published and unpublished works pertinent to the Yorkshire Dales National Park.

(xi) Further develop close liaison with specialist groups.

(xii) Develop closer liaison between the National Park Committee and District Councils, Parish Councils and Parish Meetings in the National Park.

(xiii) Encourage the general public, the press and other media to take a constructive and lively interest in the way in which the National Park Committee discharges its statutory functions.

Table 19   Yorkshire Dales National Park Plan 1977

landscape value so that policies might be developed for their enhancement or conservation, and to identify areas which are vulnerable to pressure, or which can, alternatively, accommodate change and so reduce the pressure for development in more sensitive areas. Once again, identification of high quality landscape will not guarantee that conservation interests will prevail, but it does identify a criterion against which the impact of development can be measured.

iii) Management agreements   One of the positive planning activities that local authorities may engage in which has benefit for the conservation interest is a management agreement. This is an arrangement between a local planning authority and landholders, in which in return for some form of compensation, consideration or practical assistance, the landholder agrees to safeguard certain features of the landscape, or to enhance the facilities for access to a stretch of countryside. By their nature, such agreements are site specific but their general objective is to reconcile the interests of visitors and farmers. For instance, by a combination of small financial payments, technical assistance and voluntary help, particular footpaths may be improved and waymarked, stiles and walls rebuilt so that visitors are encouraged to use these rather than other routes across farmland and open country. This has now become standard practice in many areas, in both country parks and National Parks. The link between landowners and the local authority is provided by a full-time ranger/ National Park warden, while voluntary helpers act as a supplement for visitor guidance and occasional maintenance.

Management agreements are of key importance in the preservation of field monuments, from ensuring that funerary barrows are not ploughed out to the preservation of ridge and furrow and deserted medieval village sites, or even to the maintenance of ancient (and now uneconomic) patterns of enclosure. The sort of payments which will be required may vary from small payments in kind to relatively large capital sums and regular maintenance payments. Very large scale management agreements may also include exemption from Capital Transfer Tax. For instance, 14,500 acres of open moorland at Bransdale in the North York Moors National Park were the subject of a special agreement between the landowner, the Countryside Commission, the DOE and the Nature Conservancy Council in 1982. In return for exemption, the landowner has agreed a plan to conserve and enhance landscape and wildlife, archaeological and historic sites, and to allow free access on foot and horseback, while managing the moor

for the traditional use of sheep grazing and grouse rearing in the best long-term interests of amenity.

iv) Sites of Special Scientific Interest   Under the Wildlife and Countryside Act, 1981, the Nature Conservancy Council is charged with the task of bringing to the notice of the Secretary of State and local planning authorities such sites where the flora, fauna or physiography is of particular merit and deserves safeguarding. On designation of such sites a management agreement may be entered into between the NCC, the landholder and the local authority, but the need for compensation may be very considerable, particularly if farmers are refused the normal EEC/MAFF aid for works such as the ploughing up of moorland which may affect the object of designation. In the preparation of the legislation conservation interests indicated that the level of funds would be insufficient to meet the demands for compensation, while it was feared that landholders would resist designation without very considerable compensation. Events have proved these fears to be justified and there is now a measure of agreement that the Act is not achieving its objectives. In contrast to the situation in the 1939–45 war, the maximisation of agricultural output is no longer necessary. Yet EEC policies have encouraged land improvement and intensified farming methods at the expense of 'natural' and 'traditional' landscapes. In both situations conservation legislation is swimming against the tide. The Nature Conservancy Council's budget in 1983–84, for instance, was only £12.6 millions, compared to over £1,700 millions paid out to farmers in the interests of agricultural efficiency. Both the Council for the Protection of Rural England and the Council of National Parks have represented that the Act may actually stimulate new pressures on the countryside, inducing farmers to make a case for cultivation of designated sites as a means of obtaining compensation. Yet funds are clearly inadequate to meet such needs. It was estimated in 1983, for instance, that to protect all the vulnerable marginal land in the county of Suffolk alone would cost £8 millions. The unhappy early years of this Act contrast markedly with earlier approaches where informal management agreements were negotiated, and point up very sharply the fact that best conservation practice rests ultimately upon the goodwill of occupiers, rather than the resolve of bureaucrats.

Minerals

The working of minerals has proved a contentious environmental issue not only in National Parks, but also in many other rural areas. The proposed development of the Vale of Belvoir coalfield was a well-known recent example. Planning authorities have an obligation to take account of the existence of mineral resources and the need to exploit them. They must ensure that such resources are not sterilised by other land uses, while the need to extend their use is protected by lengthening the period during which planning permission may be taken up from the customary five years to ten years. On the other hand, planning authorities must also make reviews from time to time of permissions which have not been taken up, with a view to modifying or revoking them in the light of any new circumstances. Planning permission for mineral extraction, even for existing works, is deemed to have expired after 60 years, or earlier if the planning authority so required and thereafter fresh permission must be sought. Subsequent to the Stevens Report, 1977, the Town and Country Planning Minerals Act, 1981, enables the local planning authority to make stipulations not only as to the life and manner of extractions, but also on subsequent restoration of the site including the removal of buildings and other works. This is to ensure that the major disturbance occasioned by mineral working does not interfere with the reasonable expectations of adjacent users.

Trees and Woodland

The availability of trees and woodland as both an amenity and as a reserve of timber has been of concern since Norman times, and in the present century extensive powers have been taken by central and local government to secure the provision of woodland species. As a commercial crop, standing timber is not strictly a concern of town and country planning legislation, but the planning of woodland by a central government agency dates from the establishment of the *Forestry Commission* in 1919. Such national woodlands now amount to one third of total woodland area in the country, and consist primarily of coniferous species. The resource value of such forests has been enhanced over recent years by their increased recreational use. Under the 1967 and 1968 Countryside Acts, the Forestry Commission has an obligation to consider questions of amenity in undertaking new plantings, and its woodlands may now figure prominently in recreational strategies at county or regional levels. Under the 1951 and 1967 Forestry Acts, the felling of timber may only take place under consent from the Forestry Commission, whose authority thus extends to the private sector. It is, however possible to avoid this obligation if private owners enter into a *dedication scheme*, which may apply to

existing as well as to new plantings. Under such a scheme, the owner is entitled to grant aid where he is able to demonstrate management objectives which allow for public access, nature conservation and general regard to public amenity.

Amenity aspects, however, extend beyond matters of woodland recreation, into less easily identifiable design criteria. Thus individual trees or groups of trees or even whole woods, may make a special contribution both to the urban and the rural scene. As such they may be the subject of *tree preservation orders* made under Section 60 of the 1971 Town and Country Planning Act. Such orders prohibit the felling, lopping or damage to the trees without the consent of the local planning authority, and in the case of woodland cleared for timber, may require the land to be replanted with trees. The amenity value of trees has also led to local planning authorities being obliged to consider whether to make tree preservation orders, or the planting of new trees, a condition of approval for planning applications.

8.3   AMENITY IN THE BUILT ENVIRONMENT

We have noted the more significant structural aspects of planning the built environment in the earlier chapters, but it is appropriate here to consider questions of amenity. This is largely expressed in the desire to eradicate eyesores, such as derelict land, to regulate potentially intrusive activities such as advertisements, and to conserve valued buildings or areas of cherished townscape.

Individual Buildings

Ever since the Renaissance, architectural styles of the past have been admired, although examples have only been given official protection since the Ancient Monuments Act, 1882. Since that time a small, but steadily increasing number of items have been scheduled as *ancient monuments* and taken into the care of central government. They are now the responsibility of a recently established fringe body, the *Historic Buildings and Monuments Commission*. Under the 1979 Ancient Monuments and Archaeological Areas Act it has been recognised that the setting of such remains needs to be secured as well as the remains themselves, and this is to be achieved by means of management agreements to ensure appropriate maintenance and proper public access.

Terraced buildings	2,588
Detached secular buildings	639
Churches and chapels	65
Barns, mills and other major structures	19
Minor structures (as below)	359

Gatepiers, gates and railings	105
Walls	91
Lamp posts	18
Drinking fountains	21
Statues	11
Gazebos	6
War memorials	6
Towers/chimneys	6
Stables	5
Milestones	4
Tombs	4
Garden buildings	4
Orangeries	4
Obelisks	4
Monuments	3
Balustrades	3
Powder houses	3
Bollards	3
Ironwork round Public Convenience	2
Quays	2
Walled entrance screens	2
Engine Houses	2
Vaulted chambers	2
Transit sheds	2
Bird baths	2
Tunnels	2

Plus a host of other single features from a giraffe house to a garden seat. (25 items in all).

Age of listed buildings	14th century	0.1%
	17th century	2.5
	18th century	28.0
	19th century	66.0
	20th century	2.5

Source: Planning, 315, 1979

Table 20   Analysis of listed buildings in Bristol

Criteria for conservation are much wider now than was envisaged in the nineteenth century, however, and local authorities have a duty to compile a list of buildings which they deem to be of historic, or architectural merit, or to make a special contribution to the landscape. The definition of 'building' for the purpose of the Act is very wide as is shown by the great range of features indicated in Table 20. Buildings of national importance are classified as Grade I, a category which includes only 2–3% of all buildings on the lists. Buildings which are deemed to be of special interest and deserve every effort being made to preserve them are classified as Grade II, and other notable buildings are identified as Grade II*. Entry on to the lists requires the approval of the Secretary of State for the Environment.

Listing does not guarantee preservation, but simply ensures that special interest is taken by the local planning authority in any proposed development of the building, or adjacent to it, and that such proposals are brought to the attention of the general public and such interested parties as Amenity Groups. *Listed building consent* has to be obtained from the local planning authority for any addition, alteration or for the demolition of a listed building. The local planning authority can also oblige an owner to undertake repair work in urgent cases, or may even compulsorily acquire a listed building that is in need of repair. Because of the revenue consequences to a local authority, however, this procedure is followed very rarely. Where listing is incomplete a *Building Preservation Notice* may be served to protect an endangered structure. The notice applies listed building status for six months, during which time the local authority can apply for the structure to be spot listed.

A major lacuna in the legislation, however, is the *ecclesiastical exemption*. Where a church is in use for religious worship, it can be altered or extended without listed building consent. Since there are over 20,000 such buildings, forming a major aspect of the national heritage, this is a not insignificant issue. The majority of these churches are owned by the Church of England which has a 'faculty' procedure to safeguard heritage matters, but since the increasing regard that has been given to Nonconformist and Roman Catholic church buildings in recent years (neither of which have equivalent procedures to the Church of England), there has been growing concern over ecclesiastical exemption. The issue is a thorny one, since it impinges upon the question of religious liberty. It is argued that churches in use cannot be fossilised as museum pieces, since they have been altered in the past and periodically need to be adapted to the requirements of contemporary worship.

Conservation Areas

Some buildings have a group value in terms of the character and quality of the local scene beyond any individual merit they may have, or indeed in spite of their individual lack of architectural or historic quality. The need to protect such special ensembles of buildings has been recognised in the concept of the Conservation Area. First enunciated in the Civic Amenities Act, 1967, local planning authorities are now required to identify areas of special architectural or historic interest, the character or appearance of which it is desirable to preserve or enhance. This legislation has been applied in a variety of circumstances, from a Victorian city centre to hamlets in the countryside. As is shown in Fig 8.2, conservation areas take account of the setting as well as the identity of the site under consideration, and so, for example, might include an area of agricultural land immediately adjacent to a village grouping. Protection extends beyond built structures and includes all trees within the area designated. By March 1984 over 5,000 conservation areas had been designated.

As with individual buildings, designation of a conservation area does not preclude development, but it is a means by which development can be more carefully controlled. The simple fact of designation draws attention to the special character of the area, and it is the duty of the local planning authority not only to try and ensure that new developments relate to that character, but also to draw up schemes to enhance such character, in so far as it lies within their power. Thus local planning authorities can make use of traffic control orders, facilities under housing legislation etc., as well as undertake improvement works such as tree planting and re-paving. District councils may receive additional grants in aid from county councils for such schemes and for the clearance or demolition of unsightly buildings. In addition the Secretary of State for the Environment can agree jointly to allocate sums over a period of years as grants for the repair of buildings forming a group of 'outstanding' historic or architectural interest. Costs of improvement in such *Town Schemes* are met 50% by the owner and 25% each by the local authority and the Secretary of State. Only limited funds are available, however, and in cities such as York and Chester the sums available are only a drop in the ocean given the enormity of the task. Nevertheless, the intention is to engage in positive improvements in these designated areas, rather than simply prevent unsuitable development, although it must be admitted that designation is running a long way ahead of improvement schemes in many conservation areas. An important means of guid-

Figure 8.2

Section of Almondbury Conservation Area.

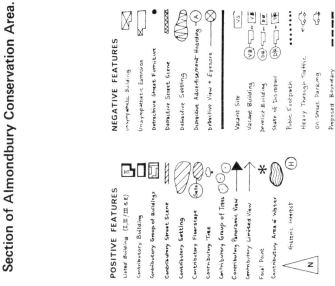

ing the outward form of development is through the preparation of *design guides* which give indications as to desirable characteristics of design appropriate for particular areas. Such guides may draw attention to the use of particular materials and such design details as pitch of roof, fenestration and landscaping. Development control is of special importance in conservation areas and the relaxation of control under the GDO 1981 does not apply to conservation areas designated at that time.

Derelict Land

The problem of derelict land has been recognised by planning legislation since the 1940's. It is a characteristic of declining industrial areas, the inner city, and most significantly of the mining and quarrying industries. Although the Derelict Land Reclamation Agency called for by the Hunt Report was never instituted, more than lip service has been paid to the problem. Since the Local Government Act, 1972, central government has been prepared to give local authorities 100% grants for reclamation works in the assisted areas and other designated *Derelict Land Clearance Areas* (areas where it is felt that such works will specifically encourage industrial regeneration), and 75% grants in AONBs and National Parks. This was by no means the first time such grant aid was made available, and subsequent legislation has widened the concept of 'derelict land' to include land which is neglected or unsightly and requiring reclamation or improvement. Much has undoubtedly been done, yet the problem remains an enormous one, not least because such grants may now form part of the block grant mechanism, and funds intended for reclamation may become diverted towards more pressing needs.

The problem is also complicated by issues of ownership, but even when derelict land is in the hand of a public body the issue remains difficult. In 1982, for instance, the Birmingham Inner City Partnership team identified no less than 726 vacant sites, totalling more than 300 ha, 80% of which was in public ownership, 50% belonging to the city council itself. The better utilisation of these sites, though, was frustrated by fragmentation and small size, many sites being under 1 ha, and only 19 being larger than 3 ha. Half the sites were affected by development constraints, and in some cases reclamation would be prohibitively expensive. Although the DOE has published plans to make government assistance more freely available, public spending restraints have frustrated their better intentions, and the problem remains acute in some areas, a lingering sore in others.

A spectacular and innovative form of reclamation was undertaken between 1981–84 by the Merseyside Development Corporation (although the idea had been under consideration for some time previous to the designation of the development corporation). In both the United States and W. Germany it had been shown that the regeneration of inner urban areas could be assisted by undertaking a substantial 'confidence-boosting' landscaping exercise. Thus 250 acres on the city's derelict waterfront were transformed into the site of the Liverpool International Garden Festival. A further site at Stoke on Trent was already under consideration at the same time, but the attention given to Merseyside by Secretary of State Heseltine ensured that Liverpool was given the first chance, and the Stoke on Trent Garden Festival is planned for 1986.

Advertisements

Travel outside the United Kingdom reveals the extent to which the control of advertisements is a marked visual feature of the British planning system. Controls of some kind have been in existence since the Advertisements Regulation Act, 1907, and they have been a feature of all planning legislation since the 1947 Act. While draft DOE advice in 1982 indicated that applicants should have their display approved unless it causes or will cause 'material injury to amenity' or a danger to public safety, much discretion remains with the district planning authority. Except in conservation areas, or other zones designated as *areas of special control*, however, no attempt is made to control the style or detail of advertisements. The strength of control, though, has been such as to curb the rash of signs that are such an intrusive feature of many other countries.

8.4 CONCLUSION

As we have seen, a great deal of environmental planning is concerned with conservation, yet such policies cannot operate in a development vacuum. Articulate cases have been made against the speed and scale of development in some National Parks, especially as they are often the result of the application of other public policy relating to water supply, forestry, reclamation of moorland and the development of mineral deposits, yet it can be argued that these are all legitimate alternative uses of the land. Similarly, it is not necessarily equitable so to restrict the range of job opportunities of the residents of such areas, that they should be obliged to live in a tastefully developed rustic museum for the sake of the amenity of their urban cousins. A similar range of problems can be seen in urban areas. Particularly in the historic city, environmental policies need to be viewed as a much wider issue than the restoration of ancient buildings and the application of appropriate cosmetic treatment. Policies relating to the maintenance of a viable central business district (often co-incident with or adjacent to the historic core), housing and traffic management will each impinge upon the needs for conservation. It is by no means easy to reconcile these various interests and provide a high standard of conservation as well as meeting the proper business needs of the community and the requirements for residential accommodation at modern standards and at reasonable cost. Nevertheless, careful maintenance of the fabric of the built environment can be achieved while pursuing other policies e.g. housing renewal, and through urban development corporation projects. It is increasingly realised that new investment is drawn to areas which are in themselves attractive, and the enhancement of both the urban and rural environment is, therefore, an important factor not only in attracting tourist-generated income, but in promoting the best interests of the whole area.

A second issue relates, once again, to the need for planners to have close liaison with the public at large. The ill-will generated by the Wildlife Act has already been contrasted with the good will which leads to the conclusion of management agreements. This needs to be secured generally as well as formally in designated areas in both town and country. A great deal rests upon the acceptance by residents and developers alike of the necessity for the highest standards of design and maintenance, and this is only going to be forthcoming if public bodies set a good example. As in so many other aspects of planning, the best results are obtained when there is an active partnership between all the parties involved, and since the 1974 Town and Country Planning (Amenities) Act, for instance, local authorities have been obliged to establish advisory committees for conservation areas to ensure proper local participation. An interesting earlier example of this is to be seen in the 'Georgian' New Town area of Edinburgh. In 1970 a Joint Committee was established composed of representatives of the New Town Residents' Association, voluntary bodies, the City of Edinburgh District Council and the Scottish Development Department. The Edinburgh New Town Conservation Committee area covers 318 ha in the city centre, containing almost 12,000 separate properties, two thirds of which are residential. The population of the area numbers c 24,000.

Since 1970 the Committee has received over £1.5 millions from central and local government for restoration purposes, but it also has an important local role to play in the provision of advice, acting as a clearing house for disposable features such as fireplaces and doorcases, and promoting the image of the area to visitors.

Lastly, we should also note that like all planning, environmental planning has social impacts. It would be true to say that the policies essentially directed towards the material environment, in both town and country, which have encouraged strict development control on the one hand and rehabilitation of existing property on the other have been of more benefit to the more prosperous sections of society than any other. Gentrification has been a marked feature of several inner urban areas as improvements to the urban fabric have reduced the amount of privately rented accommodation on the one hand and increased property values beyond the reach of local urban workers on the other. Similarly in the countryside middle class migrants have carefully restored country cottages, but at purchase, outbid local residents who are banished to council estates, perhaps in adjacent villages. Equally, insofar as rural conservation has led to the restriction of job opportunities, it has had more effect upon the indigenous young, often without transport, than on the middle class migrant who may well be retired anyway. Similarly, the encouragement given to recreation and tourism in such areas while superficially stimulating the economy, provides in its train problems of seasonality, and only adds another low-wage industry to areas which require better job opportunities if they are to retain a cross section of the younger population. By these means, therefore, apparent improvements may well conceal disbenefits, and the personal and communal implications of such policies raises yet again the serious question: who is planning for whom?

Further reading

A good overview of the problems of planning in rural areas is offered by M Blacksell & A W Gilg 1981 in *The Countryside: planning and change* (George Allen & Unwin). National park plans are reviewed by A Dennier 1978 in *Town Planning Review* 49, but for a vigorous critique of policies in national parks see A & M MacEwen 1982 *National Parks: conservation or cosmetics?* (George Allen & Unwin). In equally spirited fashion G Moss 1981 reviews *Britain's Wasted Acres: land use in a changing society* (Architectural Press). A Coleman's critique of the land-use implications of post-war planning will be found in *Architects' Journal* (January 1977). For examples of conservation policies and practice, two useful case studies are given by D W Inall 1982 *Conservation in Action: Chester's Bridgegate* (HMSO) and J F Wager 1981 *Conservation of Historic Landscapes in the Peak District National Park* (Peak Park Joint Planning Board) and from the same source comes J Wager 1978 *Management Agreements in Principle and Practice: a case study of Monsal Dale, Bakewell*. There is a considerable literature on landscape evaluation, but the special edition of *Landscape Research* 1981 Vol 6 pt 2 is devoted to the subject and carries several useful articles on both theory and practice.

CONCLUSION

Planning in Britain is most obviously characterised by a pragmatic approach. It originated as a set of activities designed to ameliorate the unacceptable environmental and social consequences of the operation of the market economy. As such it stands in the British tradition of liberal regulation largely operated at the local level under a degree of central supervision. By this same token, British planning contains an internal contradiction. 'Planning' assumes at most, control over that which is to happen, or at least, an ability to identify aims and objectives for the future; but such is not the nature of the British political system. Thus, while planners may be assumed to have the competence to plan, the national structures within which planning operates neither enables them to do so, nor provides them with plainly articulated goals. Planning in Britain is therefore largely confined to a set of technical procedures operated in response to local requirements.

The basic machinery of the planning system was reviewed in Part One. It is clear that the technical procedures of planning are highly complex. They are the fruits of a corps of professionals who in response to the open-ended nature of their brief, have developed and enlarged upon the area of their operation. It could be argued that the more planners there are, the more problems will be identified which will require more planners and procedures for their solution. This indeed seemed to be the case, for the profession expanded rapidly between the report of the Planning Advisory Group in 1965 and the re-organisation of local government in 1974. Planning appeared to have become pre-occupied with technical procedures and to be paying less attention to the formulation of goals and objectives. Planning, in short, seemed in the 1960's and 1970's to be in danger of becoming an end in itself.

In order to remedy this situation, planners are being drawn into closer interaction with the various activities they are supposed to plan for. This has seemed to be most realistically done at district level where developers and planners can be involved in dialogue as to the acceptability of development proposals. Whether this makes a call upon informal planning methods and use of planning gain or not, it is a logical step in pragmatic planning. Elsewhere, planners have been accused of failing to understand real-world requirements, as (Chapter 6) they have sought to maintain existing patterns of retailing, trying to ensure that shopping conforms to theoretical models, rather than understanding that the distribution industry was in the process of being transformed.

Problems of inter-action and co-ordination occur not just with particular development proposals, however, but lie at the heart of the whole machinery of planning. Part One describes how local planning authorities do not find it easy to interpret the policy intentions of central government as put out in circulars, ministerial decisions and the recommendations of the inspectorate. In Chapter 5 we described how shifting and ambiguous central stances towards the question of public transport facilities made long term transportation planning difficult on the part of local authorities. Thus there are difficulties in interpreting central policies, which themselves may conflict in their implications from one department to another. Local planners may experience further difficulty in accommodating the variety of land use demands made by individual local authority departments, over whose plans for financial commitment they have no control. This should be easier in those local authorities where planners have been involved in some form of corporate planning and where, say at county level, the structure plan provides a strategic guide. Beyond the formal structure, though, we described in Chapter 8 how planning objectives as regards conservation could best be met by harnessing the willing co-operation of private owners. If planners appear to be over-concerned with the processes of planning, rather than its purposes, therefore, it is not surprising, since its processes are so deviously labyrinthine.

As we have surveyed the scope of planning, it is quite clear that the actual powers vested in the planning system labour under more constraints than might be popularly imagined. Despite the impressive range of legislation and procedures described in Part One, there are few effective means of positive planning. With a few exceptions such as the New Town Development Corporations and the new Urban Development Corporations, planners do not have the means to ensure the materialization of their plans, since their major functions are limited to the preparation of development plans and to permitting or restricting development proposals. Unfortunately even plan preparation and development control have become divorced from each other (Chapter 3), rendering the former less meaningful. In reality, there is little control over 'development' at all, except insofar as initial planning permission may be given, refused or given conditionally. Just as planning is rarely in a position to elicit development, so can it do little to control any existing legitimate activities, however 'inappropriate' they might become. Most notably in Chapter 4 we saw the weakness of planning's positive powers. Since in this regard planning rests upon development control, it is obviously weakened when little development takes place as in a time of recession. At local level attempts to engage in economic regeneration are frustrated by the ambiguity of the role of local authorities in such a task along with a lack of funds. By the provision of space and facilities a planning authority can enable economic development to occur, but it can do little to ensure its occurrence. Even in the most comprehensively planned environments of all, the new towns, economic success seems to have more to do with the general prosperity of the region than the best efforts of the planners.

If the scope of planning is more limited than the term planning might imply, its success is a rather more open-ended question. At a local level it is certainly possible to point to individual planning successes, related to its regulatory function, particularly in specific acts of conservation in both urban and rural areas. Equally it is possible to identify obvious disasters, not least in the field of housing provision. But this is to view planning in pragmatic terms only, and it is not easy to identify broader criteria against which planning's success can be measured. Planning policies have a social context and social consequences. While planning is a technical process, it is also an attempt to make judgements on behalf of the community as to what is or is not acceptable and appropriate development. We can see these judgements being made at every planning level. The very act of structure planning demands choice as to what seems to be a desirable state of affairs, tempered by awareness of such external factors as the state of the national economy, and the reality of present conditions. Local plans are similarly conceived with the intention of at least best

satisfying local requirements for land, and both these and structure plans require a measure of public participation to help identify what 'best' might mean for different social groups. In development control (Chapter 2), each case must be dealt with on its individual merits but both objective and subjective criteria come into play. While standard procedures will be followed for each application, at the end of the day a judgement has to be made either on the part of officers or elected members which will be informed not just by the technical merits of the case but also by some notion as to what is a desirable goal; this may be a matter of taste in design or an overt or covert political gain. Indeed, the political side may loom larger in the light of the re-distribution of costs and benefits which almost inevitably follow on from a planning decision.

Whether desirable goals are identified via public participation, elected members, the Secretary of State, the DOE or local planners, there has been little public debate as to what they should be. This is surprising, since planning is inevitably political in nature, for according to planning policies and decisions, benefits may be given or taken away from members of the public. This lack of debate and agreement is most obvious in the fact that there is no 'national development plan', and since the dismemberment of the regional economic planning councils, no publicly accepted regional strategy. Also, there is little obvious correlation between the structure planning process and the wide array of other types of plan making by other departments of local authorities etc (Fig 9.1). Indeed the range of plans is such as to be beyond the coordination of the centre, certainly not by the DOE alone, since much planning relates to the work of other Departments of State. Without such an overall view of planning, it is not easy to evaluate its success. The 'town planner' of the 1920's might have measured success in terms of the salubrious suburb. The 'urban and regional planner' of the 1960's might have been concerned with criteria of 'efficiency' particularly in the movement of goods and people within the urban hierarchy. The 'environmental planner' in more recent times might use more wide ranging criteria which are closer to the aspirations of those who sought the establishment of the present planning system in the 1930's and 1940's. In some senses we can see these forming the received wisdom of what planning is all about although they are not supported by an exactly formulated body of theory and are not necessarily mutually supporting. We can summarise these criteria as being on the one hand resource based, and on the other socially based.

Resource based views of planning's purposes would be

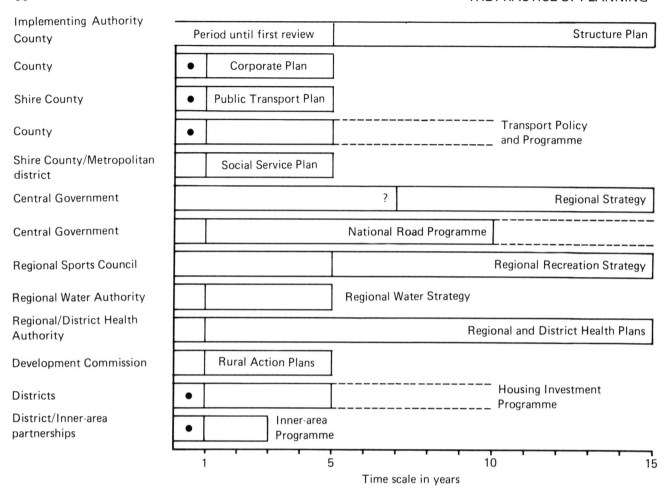

Figure 9.1   Structure plans and other statutory plan-making

concerned with issues such as the containment of urban sprawl and the conservation of high quality agricultural land. Social based views of planning would be concerned with the amelioration of living conditions, especially for those least able to improve their own, and for the provision of an appropriate array of civic amenities. Both views would probably contain reference to the protection of amenity as discussed in Chapter 8. Such goals would probably be regarded as legitimate by most planners although there might well be more argument about the means to achieve them. Even those in the development industry most vociferous in their criticism of the planning system would probably concede the appropriateness of such goals, for their criticism has been mainly directed towards the efficiency of the

system rather than its purposes. Yet if these are the unwritten goals, it could be argued that after almost forty years planning has not met with notable success. The rates of both urban expansion and contraction of agricultural land have hardly changed for the better since 1947. The net result of policies designed to provide spanking new comprehensively developed town centres and disperse crowded urban populations to peripheral housing estates and new towns; to protect the countryside; or to rehabilitate the historic city have been of more benefit to the mobile and affluent middle class, than to the socially deprived. No policy decisions were taken deliberately to achieve such a result, yet such has been the upshot of a well-intentioned system in the context of the considerable economic, social and

INFLUENTIAL REPORTS 1963–69

1963   **Buchanan Report** – Traffic in Towns.
1965   **Abel-Smith & Townsend** – The Poor and the Poorest, **Milner Holland Report** – Housing in
        Greater London, **Planning Advisory Group** – The Future of Development Plans.
1966   **Dennington Report** – Our Holder Homes – a call for action.
1967   **Plowden Report** Children and their Primary Schools, **Maud Report** – Management of Local
        Government, **National Committee for Commonwealth Immigrants** – Areas of Special Housing Need.
1968   **Seebohm Report** – Local Authority and Allied Personal Social Service.
1969   **Skeffington Report** – People and Planning.

CENTRAL INITIATIVES 1968–77

1968   Home Office launches Urban Programme, Department of Education Educational Priority Areas
        Research (Deptford, Birmingham, Conisbrough, Liverpool and Dundee).
1969   Home Office launches Community Development Projects in Liverpool, Glamorgan, Coventry,
        Southwark, Newham, Newcastle, West Riding, Cumberland, Birmingham, Paisley, Tynemouth
        and Oldham.
1971   Home Office launches Neighbourhood Schemes in Liverpool and Teesside.
1972   DOE produces Urban Guidelines (Sunderland, Oldham and Rotherham) and Inner Area Studies
        (Birmingham, Liverpool and Lambeth).
1973   Department of Health and Social Security undertakes Cycle of Deprivation Studies.
1974   Home Office introduces Comprehensive Community Programmes. (Motherwell, Gateshead and
        Bradford) DOE introduces Area Management Trials (Liverpool, Newcastle, Middlesbrough,
        Islington, Haringey, Dudley, Stockport, Kirklees).
1977   The Inner Areas debate and launch of Policy for the Inner Cities under the general supervision of
        the DOE.

INNER URBAN AREAS ACT 1978

1978   Inner Urban Areas Act designated – **7 partnership authorities** comprising Birmingham, Liverpool,
        Manchester/Salford, Newcastle/Gateshead, Lambeth, Hackney/Islington, London Docklands
        (Greenwich, Lewisham, Newham, Southwark, Tower Hamlets).
                                – **15 programme authorities** – Bolton, Bradford, Hammersmith,
        Hull, Leeds, Leicester, Middlesbrough, North Tyneside, Nottingham, Oldham, Sheffield, South
        Tyneside, Sunderland, Wirral, Wolverhampton.
                                – **19 'other districts'** – Barnsley, Blackburn, Brent, Doncaster,
        Ealing, Haringey, Hartlepool, Rochdale, Rotherham, St. Helens, Sandwell, Sefton, Wandsworth,
        Wigan, Blaenau Gwent, Cardiff, Newport, Rhondda, Swansea.
        All designated areas given powers to make loans/grants and declare improvement areas in
        accordance with 'programmes' of action. Differential level of government assistance made available
        in above order of priority. Most central government departments involved together with a range
        of local government agencies, including planning departments.

CENTRAL INITIATIVES 1980–83

1980   Local Government Planning & Land Act introduces Enterprise Zones and Urban Development
        Corporations.
1981   Appointment of Minister with special responsibility for Merseyside; Scarman Report on The
        Brixton Disorders; Financial Institutions Group created (private sector financiers seconded
        to DOE).
1982   New style of urban development grant for Partnership; Programme and Designated other districts;
        Pump priming grants for Urban Programme Projects or Derelict Land Programmes;
        Inner City Enterprise established – a service company funded by financial institutions to identify
        potential inner city investments.
1983   Urban Development and Derelict Land Grants allocated; Designation of new Programme
        Authorities: Blackburn, Brent, Coventry, Knowlsey, Rochdale, Sandwell, Tower Hamlets,
        Wandsworth; Declaration of new Designated Districts: Walsall, Langbaurgh, Burnley;
        Appointment of Minister with special responsibility for the West Midlands.

Source: after M S Gibson and M J Langstaff (1982) *An Introduction to Urban Renewal* Hutchinson.

Table 21   Inner City Initiatives

technological changes which have occurred over the same period.

Many of these points are illustrated by the seemingly intractable problems of the inner city. Town and country planning is certainly partly to blame for the carnage wrought by slum clearance and redevelopment, and the loss of population and industry as a result of inflexible zoning and new town and regional policies. Yet one of the redeeming features of the ill-fated Community Development Projects (1975) was the identification of a wider set of reasons for inner city decline, including the operation of the capital market, and the failure of the welfare state to deal properly with social need as well as misguided (and under-financed) planning policies. Nevertheless, as Table 21 shows the inner city has not been without close study since the 1960's and considerable amounts of public investment have been made. By 1982–3, government aid on inner city projects, including the Liverpool and London Docklands urban development corporation projects, had reached £415 millions p.a., disbursed in a myriad ways. The seven inner city partnerships (Birmingham, Hackney, Islington, Lambeth, Liverpool, Newcastle-Gateshead and Salford), for instance, which bring together central and local government, chambers of commerce and voluntary organisations, have placed 39% of their funds in social schemes, 36% in economic investment and 25% in environmental improvements, yet the inter-relationships between these various activities are very imperfectly understood. The hope is that private enterprise will follow the lead of public investment in a revival of the inner city. However even to speak of revival is to look backwards and not to think innovatively in terms of the future.

In the event, considerable gains have been made at the local level, particularly in the matter of co-ordination of effort and pointing to the way in which local planning can be much more positively integrated into the development process, but this is less so at the centre. It seems doubtful that the problems of the inner city can possibly be solved by policies aimed solely at the inner city. Their problems have arisen because of movement out of the city into peripheral and even distant locations, so it would seem logical to take a wider view. In terms of the largest cities and the conurbations this would almost certainly mean a regional perspective within an overall national strategy. If the sums available for urban aid were added to those for regional aid and the various training schemes operated by the Manpower Services Commission, for instance, over £2½ billions would have been available for social and economic regener-

ation in 1982–3. This massive total was spent with little regard to any broader strategic purpose simply because inter-departmental co-ordination was of such a low order that there was no effective mechanism for the formulation of a national development strategy.

It is inevitable that in such circumstances, planning, like much of public policy-making, should remain incremental and reactive in character, falling far short of the hopes pinned on it by its early proponents. This should not necessarily be seen as a failure, for it simply reflects the nature of the British polity in the early 1980's. While the economy may be mixed, liberty remains the touchstone. This despite the extent of the state's control of the public services in central and local government, its massive spending power and its involvement in a wide variety of economic enterprises. 'National planning' does not have a notable record of success in the command economies of the Soviet bloc, so we might have even less expectation of its performance in Britain, dependent as it is on the fortunes of the world economy. Planning in Britain remains an activity largely bound by the status quo, yet obliged to take a view of the future. Even if it has imperfectly formulated ends, planning certainly has consequences and in these and its means it has both technical and political aspects. Planners are often forced into value choices when many would prefer them to remain technical experts, yet until politicians themselves articulate what shape they would wish for the future, planners must either remain trapped by the present, or take unto themselves that identification of goals for which they are unfitted, and unable of themselves, to achieve.

Further reading

A vast amount of literature exists on planning theory and its evolution. The following edited volumes provide concise readings on alternative theoretical perspectives; P Healey G McDougall & M J Thomas 1982 *Planning Theory: prospects for the 1980's* (Pergamon) C Paris 1982 *Critical Readings in Planning Theory* (Pergamon). A very useful sociological analysis of the planning system can be found in E Reade 1982 The British planning system, Unit 19 *Open University Course D202 (Urban Change and Conflict)*. A Ravetz 1980 shows the evolution of planning theory and its impact on the urban scene in *Remaking Cities* (Croom Helm), while probably the best comprehensive coverage of inner city problems is to be found in P Lawless 1981 *Britain's Inner Cities: problems and policies* (Harper & Row).

INDEX